Cutoffs

Cutoffs

How Family Members Who Sever Relationships Can Reconnect

By Carol Netzer

NEW HORIZON PRESS   FAR HILLS, NJ

Requests for permission should be addressed to:
New Horizon Press
P.O. Box 669
Far Hills, NJ 07931

Netzer, Carol
    Cutoffs: How Family Members Who Sever Relationships Can Reconnect.

Library of Congress Catalog Card Number: Pending

ISBN: 0-88282-138-5

New Horizon Press

Manufactured in the U.S.A.

2000 1999 1998 1997 1996 / 5 4 3 2 1

For Jenny

Surgeons must be very careful
When they take the knife!
Underneath their fine incisions
Stirs the Culprit—*Life*!

—*Emily Dickinson*

CONTENTS

Acknowledgments *viii*

Author's Note *ix*

Introduction *1*

Part I, *Cutting Off* 5

1   The Frequency of Cutting Off *7*

2   The Process of Estrangement *14*

3   Cutoffs in the Family *40*

4   Famed Families Who Cut Off *66*

5   Adoption: The Severed Connection *85*

6   Cutting Off During Divorce *104*

7   Parents and Children After Divorce *124*

8   An Absolute Need to Cut Off: Incest or "Incest" *147*

9   Retrieved Memory and Cutting Off *161*

Part II, *Reconnection* *171*

10   Bridges from Cutoffs *173*

11   Healing the Split *189*

12   The Beginning of Reconnection: Ellen and Meg Revisited *214*

Epilogue *230*

References *239*

ACKNOWLEDGMENTS

Thanks to Lorraine Alexson for meticulous editing, endless patience and tact. We started as intimate strangers at work on a manuscript we both cared about and ended as friends. I am grateful to Ann Bishop for her passionate reading, her eye for gibberish, and her feeling for the exact word. Thanks to Dick Netzer for his clear sense of organization, his many hours of technical help, and his unfailing support. Scott Peck taught me to keep trying.

The work of Christopher Bollas, Masud Kahn, Melanie Klein, Arnold Modell, Thomas Ogden, Jeffrey Seinfeld, and DWW Winnicott were of great help to me.

I am grateful to Jane Fixman, Marilyn La Monica, and Harvey Pitkin for reading parts of the manuscript and commenting on it. A special thanks to Selma Zimmerman, another passionate advocate. She was always in my corner. And thanks, too, to my dog, Duffy, best friend and ideal companion. He was attentive to long monologues and alert to Fed Ex.

AUTHOR'S NOTE

This book is based on both my research and extensive interviews. In order to protect the identity of others, I have changed people's names and identifying characteristics. The conversations portrayed in this book have been reconstructed.

INTRODUCTION

We all know the story of the prodigal son, the aggrieved young man who wanted "out" of his family. The son took his inheritance, cut all family ties, and went off alone on a journey of self-exile, causing great pain to his father. Unfortunately, not much has changed since that story was told. A similar unhappy separation is just as likely to happen to a family today. It has happened to me. Perhaps it has happened to you. It is a process which I call "cutting off."

A cutoff in a family is immediately recognizable when it happens. There is a decisive leave-taking by one or more family members which puts an abrupt end to normal family relations and the survivors are left to suffer the loss.

Cutting off is common in families of all classes and backgrounds. Exactly what happens and why are usually mysteries to the participants. Why should a woman of twenty-seven suddenly stop speaking to her parents? Why should a man who has divorced his wife also stop seeing his children?

In this book I describe many kinds of cutoffs. I describe the symptoms which lead to cutting off and tell how family members can identify a cutoff when it happens. Finally, I suggest ways to repair cutoffs after they have occurred. Even when a cutoff seems to be final and irrevocable, there are steps that a family can take to bring about reconnection. The methods I describe have been used successfully by others. I believe that they will also work for you. I hope that by using them you will be able to reconnect with your loved one and to celebrate his or her return with an emotional feast as warm and forgiving as the banquet given by the biblical father upon the return of his lost son.

I come from a family of cutoffs. My mother cut off from her sister and from me, her daughter. She cut off from two grandchildren by inadvertence and from a third grandchild by fiat. (The child was my brother's son, and my brother had cut off from him.) My mother also cut off from all of her great-grandchildren. My brother cut off from me. My brother's children cut off from me. In my own nuclear family, my younger daughter cut off from me and from her father and her sister.

As I lost one person after another in my life I was forced either to learn as much as I could to combat what was happening or face even more bewildering loss in the future. I could not understand why my family was out of control. It took ten years before I figured out that cutting off occurs both in the individual who leaves and in the family who stays. The process interlocks for both parties. I learned that the process can start with either the family or the individual. And I learned that no matter who starts it, everyone feels its effects. In this book I talk about individuals and families, both singly and together. I often describe events which happened with my own family. In these descriptions, either an individual or the family will usually be in the foreground.

One of the many things I learned is that families use cutting off as a way to handle tension. When unmanageable pressure builds, they resolve it by expelling a member. They create a scapegoat to blame and end the situation. When cutting off is a family's only means of resolving conflict, the principal concern of the family is centered on orchestrating the next cutoff. Cutting off becomes the business of the family. When this is the case, everyone in the family becomes a potential black sheep to everyone else in the family. The underlying threat becomes, "If things go wrong between us, one of us is out."

Family members who live under this threat often face an individual dilemma in the cutting-off process. Some individuals are simply expelled by the others. Other individuals may elect to remove themselves, and the torment of doing this may become so great that they finally choose the most violent cutoff, that of suicide. In a macabre way, suicides stay loyal to the family business by taking upon themselves the most drastic form of self-expulsion as a way to help the family solve its conflict.

Families that live by cutting off are all extreme cases. Cutting off is their only leverage of negotiation. Normal families sometimes cut off a member too, but they are adaptive enough to nurture and negotiate without taking the final step. A family whose business it is to cut off in a pathological way cannot negotiate.

Looking at the way the extreme family behaves makes it easier for us to recognize paler forms of cutting off when they occur in ordinary families. An example would be the normal family where a parent cuts off one of the children for an infraction of family rules. The other children usually go along passively with the parent, whom they see as all-powerful, out of an unconscious fear that one of them may be next. In the extreme, rigid family, however, this fear is acted out by the other children because they know that anyone at all can be expelled and that one expulsion soon follows another.

When my brother was threatening to cut off from me about ten years ago, I went to see a family therapist whose specialty was difficult families. Cutting off is a well-known behavior in family therapy, although it rarely appears in the index of any family therapy textbook. I made a library search and turned up nothing at all: no statistics, no literature, nothing. Nor did my therapist offer me much hope. He was reading one of three letters that my brother had directed his daughter to write to me on his behalf. "As poison pen letters go," the therapist said, "this one is mild. I've got a drawer full of notes like it," he went on. "It's a regular cottage industry."

I pointed out to him that the cutting off was all on my side of the family. "My husband Dick's family bickers and backbites and tells stories on one another, and yet they all stay together," I told him.

"Garden variety family, huh?" he commented.

It was this therapist who also told me that cutting off as a solution in my own family may have begun early in this century when my grandfather went back to the "old country" to visit his first family. He was caught there by the First World War and did not return to America for many years. My grandmother and her daughters had to struggle to survive in their new country and felt abandoned by their husband and father. In their situation, emigration had created a cutoff from the familiar which was compounded by my grandfather's failure to return on time.

The therapist told me flatly that there was nothing I could do. My family was too far gone in the cutoff business. Our family structure was too corroded to be fixed. Like an oracle, he warned me that a cutoff would probably happen again, since cutting-off families tend to expel even more members in the next generation. It seemed to me that he was talking as if we had an emotional virus. This was so similar to my own thoughts that I told him so. He agreed and told me that the strain tends to become more virulent with each new generation. "You see the same mechanism in feuding families in the back hills of Appalachia and in Bosnia," he said. "It only gets worse."

PART I

Cutting Off

PART 1

1

THE FREQUENCY
OF CUTTING OFF

Cutting off is a widespread phenomenon. Though unnamed in psychology books, it is recognizable and inherent in certain life events such as death, divorce and remarriage, adoption, and emigration.

For example, we have been especially slow to identify the lingering disruption of divorce upon children, although we have seen how children of divorcing parents are often used as bargaining chips, and how sometimes one parent cuts off or grows distant. Sadly, this scenario is all too familiar. Everyone knows someone who refuses to see a divorced father or mother, who refuses to go home again, who will never speak to a brother or sister, who has been pushed out of the family, or who will not allow grandparents to see their grandchildren.

Although these family breakdowns are seen most obviously in divorce, they occur in other kinds of cutoffs as well. For example, lunching with a man I knew, I mentioned that I was writing this book. He sprang up from his seat. "I know!" he said. "That's what my sister did to me when our mother died!"

Cutting off is a deviant form of separation, that universal

process which we all experience. The difference is that cutting off is an abbreviated version of separation which omits closure on the old love or the old life. Although cutting off is an unconscious flight whose aim is to leave the past behind and start clean, it does not usually complete the job. Before one can remarry, one must separate emotionally from the old marriage. Before one can accept a stepfather, one must come to terms with the natural father one wants never to see again.

Those left behind may not want the cutoff to happen. Indeed, they may oppose it. Yet, in spite of themselves, they find that their lives have been irrevocably changed because of it. Cutting off is not a private act without consequences to others. It is like cutting a cord in two where one person's willed departure leaves the other person emotionally dangling. The reverse is true as well. Families often cut off from an individual, leaving her or him severed from the group and helpless to reconnect. This may occur as a voluntary act or as a result of a catastrophe.

The Emerging Cutoff

Whether a cutoff is the result of a long-festering grievance come to a head or of a catastrophe, the outcome (separation) is always the same. However, the process of getting there is entirely different. The cutoff usually occurs after a major change in the family, such as a marriage, a birth, or a death. The change realigns family relationships and provides a convenient coverup for the cutoff. For example, the death of a parent is often the occasion for one adult sibling to cut off from another. The estranged family member has been unconsciously heading toward cutting off anyway, following an emotional course that has its own impetus and cannot be halted. For that family member, the pot has already boiled over. The parent's death provides the pretext to act on these feelings.

Many people are fooled by the pretext for the cutoff, which might be a petty dispute over the disposal of family property. ("You took the little blue lamp in the living room!") Those who are fooled really believe that such a dispute is reason enough to say goodbye forever. They can only marvel at their sister's greed and cupidity, not realizing that the cutoff was bound to happen no matter how the property was divided, for a cutoff in the making has its own timetable. In one way this is a source of hope for families where cutoffs occur: if a cutoff is inevitable, it follows that there may be a way to prevent it from happening if we can only recognize its symptoms.

The Symptoms of a Cutoff

For the person doing it, cutting off has its own momentum. The final leave-taking seems imperative to him or her and probably cannot be prevented as it is occurring, but there are usually symptoms before a cutoff actually occurs. Months or years before departure, the brother who is cutting off from his sister, the spouse who is leaving the marriage, the fifteen-year-old who is running away, or the young adult who is joining a cult, all stop investing emotionally in those they will leave behind.

All voluntary cutoffs occur in a condition of psychic isolation. All are defensive acts against connection. All need to remain hidden and unfound. Unrelatedness is the message.

There are various ways for other family members to recognize psychic isolation. There may be a lack of initiative by the unconnected person in undertaking usual family pursuits. There may be compliance instead of active interest in a project. There may be mechanical speech and unusual silences in conversation. Another clue is the "feel" of personal interactions with the person. When you are made to feel isolated and alone in the presence of someone you think you know well, it is often because the other person is withdrawing and isolating you. For example, those who are unrelated often show a false front. They are the people who go along for the ride and never express their own preferences. They are passive and docile. Their replies are compliant; they say "Uh-huh, uh-huh" without warmth or interest. That is because they relate only to themselves. They do not initiate relationships because they have long ago vacated the field and retreated inside themselves. Forced to "relate" or interact with others, an unrelated person responds like an automaton who passively awaits signals from the outside world on how to behave, and then delivers a performance on cue. For that reason, all interaction with the unrelated person feels hollow to other people, even when a response is right.

The Feelings That Make Cutoffs Cut Off

Why would anyone withdraw in this manner? What makes a person shut down and leave their family permanently?

Usually, these people have a heightened sense of being different and alone, misunderstood, and humiliated. They have many grievances and feel unappreciated by others. They see no way out. As they see it, the road is blocked at every turn; they fear isolation but fear being controlled by others even more. They are always trying to find the right emotional distance between themselves and the rest of the family group. There seems no solution to their paradox: either others are too cold and make them feel isolated, or the others are too suffocating and make them feel controlled. These "others" push unrelated people in too close or demonstrate that they do not really want them near at all. No one can reach unrelated people in a way that feels right to them. Nor can they reach out. Because of their need to remain hidden and unfound in the busy family atmosphere, they feel safer alone. This is a circular process with no exit, and so their sense of frustration, isolation, and rage increases since no one succeeds in making contact with them in the right way. As rage mounts, their grievances grow. They become more sensitive to the ways in which they are being humiliated, and more silent. They observe how others are preferred over them and they count all the new ways others have found to exclude them.

Feeling so alone all the time, they rehearse their grievances. As the list grows longer, they become even more guarded in their interactions with "the other side," for each contact adds a new humiliation. Other people live in a different world altogether, and there really is no one unrelated people can speak to out there. Why should they even bother? Also, there is no one who has even noticed that their way is entirely different; this makes it easier to project onto those insensitive outsiders the anger and doubts and all the bad feelings which the unrelated experience. There is not one of those other people who could share this special feeling and certainly not one of them who realizes that the unrelated are special. The unrelated feel hurt and wronged by the willful ignorance of all those who are blind to their needs.

The sense of having been humiliated and wronged is an active spur to make the final break with the family. The only way out of the dilemma of feeling either alone with others or controlled by them is to leave the group. As grievances against the family mount, the person doing the cutoff finds it easier to feel that the family is wrong now and has always been wrong. It is amazing to them that they had not noticed it before. It may be the one thing they can grow passionate about.

This division of good and bad is what therapists call "splitting." Splitting is the essential action for cutting off. In the psyche, good feelings are split from bad ones. Bad feelings about "bad" people go together; good feelings about "good" people also go together.

The person's own "difference" becomes a special and superior difference. Through denial and dissociation (a "forgetting" wherein the rest of the family become nonpersons), he or she is able to withdraw from the nonpersons because of their failings. A person about to cut off believes that the family members have brought their ills on themselves with every new day bringing more evidence of their shortcomings. In this new and heady state of lonely perfection, the dissociating person's grandiosity grows unassailable. He or she has reached the point of final cutoff.

Who Cuts Off and Why

Psychic pain is hard to bear. A major loss such as the death of a parent is a time of potential cutoff because the bereaved child, even if an adult, feels better being angry than heartbroken. While we might feel guilty being angry at the dead, we feel justification in being angry at siblings, especially if we secretly hold grievances that go back to childhood. Whether we realize it consciously or not, it is much easier to cut off our siblings than to face our rage and pain at the loss of a parent. Cutting off provides our psyches with a distraction from the normal grieving process, which then does not move beyond denial and anger. Flight, avoidance, and denial are stubborn and powerful human defenses.

Grown siblings often say, "Mom kept the family together, but none of us kept in touch after she died." They say the same about their father and speak as though the dissolution of the family was a natural consequence of parental loss. The dead parent is cut off rather than mourned because mourning hurts too much. It is not hard to see how this happens. Coming together as a family to celebrate an event several months after the death of a parent only serves as a reminder that the parent is missing, and so it is avoided. Soon everyone has an excuse for not going home for Christmas anymore. It is an unconscious reaction to loss to cut off since those who remain cannot give a name to the pain without experiencing more pain. It is a simple fact. Two grown brothers might, in effect, collude in avoiding grief and break up the family over a trifle. The pain and grief that each feels are then displaced by the anger and outrage each feels toward the other. Thus death, the absolute physical cutoff, becomes an emotional cutoff for the living as well, and at a heavy price.

As we know, people have different levels of tolerance for physical and emotional pain. A woman I know feels that she ought not speak to her husband about their daughter's multiple sclerosis, because he cannot tolerate the pain. So she bears it alone. Again, avoidance and denial aid that husband's emotional flight.

It has been documented that many people are able to function if they can avoid particular events and situations that are upsetting to them, and so, they cut off.

2

THE PROCESS OF
ESTRANGEMENT

Several years ago, Ellen Sutton, a dark, wiry, and intense woman, came to see me. She had been a medical writer for several years after graduating from Smith College, and research into hereditary illness led to her interest in schizophrenia. She went back to college and, while her children were growing up, she got a doctorate in psychology.

Ellen knew from a friend that not only was I interested in cutoffs, but I had experienced them in my family. She told me, with spirit, "We are in the same boat. I want to teach you something, and I want to learn what you have to teach me." This is her case history.

Her adopted daughter Meg, who was twenty-five at the time, was a medical writer like Ellen. Meg had married a foreign student while she was an undergraduate and divorced him the next year when she found out that he had tuberculosis of the scrotum and could never have children. Meg was good at her work but she had run into trouble with editors and had left several jobs because she could not get along with people. She remarried after college and had her first child within a year. The trouble started during her pregnancy. Ellen told me the story in detail.

The Process of Estrangement

When Meg cut off from the family, she did it abruptly. One day she was Ellen's daughter, and the next day she was not. This portion of her life had simply ended, and that was that. The cutoff was impersonal and automatic, as though she and her family had no history together, as though twenty-five years of affectionate connection had never been, as though she had never had a mother, father, and brother. A blip on an imaginary computer had wiped out a file, and suddenly they were strangers.

What happened to their family was something like the experience of another client of mine, Rose, when her father became senile. For thirty-five years they had shared the warmest bond possible, depending on each other's love to see them through difficult situations. All at once Rose was to him an impudent, intrusive stranger. A Shakespearean scholar, Rose's father retained that memory and told her cuttingly, "I know you not."

Meg, too, knew her mother not. There was no relationship between them anymore. Without warning, the tie between them unraveled, but Ellen could not forget Meg. Forgotten by her daughter, however, her own existence grew dimmer. Ellen felt she too was in danger of disappearing.

Meg showed typical cutoff symptoms. If Meg and Ellen were by themselves in a room, Ellen felt as though she were alone. Making conversation was like pushing a boulder uphill. Meg did not ask anything of her mother. When Ellen asked Meg something, Meg's answers were short and phrased in such a way that they never gave rise to other questions or reflections. The world they inhabited together was concrete, flat, and devoid of color. It felt like a moonscape. Time stood still. Meg would not relate, she could not relate, to her mother. She would not speak, and she would not hear. Deep into herself, she seemed obtuse, and yet Ellen knew that her obtuseness had nothing to do with lack of intelligence because Meg's IQ was very high. Such a state is a defense against connection and provides a way of remaining

15

hidden and unfound. The person cutting off feels that she must not show herself. This is what is called the "cocoon defense."

Urelatedness: The Cocoon and the Belljar

Meg had sealed herself under a psychological belljar by putting what seemed like a glass shield between her mother and herself. Meg was there in view, but no matter how hard Ellen looked into the belljar, Meg would not look out. She would not be found. She closed down.

At one point, Ellen remembered from her studies reading something by Arnold Modell, a psychoanalyst, about people who live in a cocoon. "The cocoon is like a fortress where nothing leaves or enters. It is not only that they [those inside] do not communicate, but also that they do not hear the communications of others; they do not hear what is said to them." That was really how Ellen knew that Meg had gone. Meg did not hear her mother's voice anymore; she did not see her in her mind's eye; she did not carry her mother within her.

Meg did not call Ellen or her father, Will. Although Ellen kept writing to her, hoping to strike a spark, Meg never answered those letters. Ellen and Will had to beg to visit, and Meg only rarely consented.

The Beginning of Estrangement

The process of estrangement began late in Meg's pregnancy. As the time of the birth approached, Meg seemed to grow depressed. She was grave, low-keyed, sometimes blank and removed. Her mother thought often of a self-portrait Meg had painted in her early teens. It hangs in their living room, and Meg stares out of it, full front, unblinking, and sad. When she looked at it or thought of it, Ellen felt reproached.

Meg was still dispirited at a baby shower that her mother-in-law Dorothy gave for her a few weeks before Jane was born. She could barely bring herself to open the beautifully wrapped presents. She seemed to be sleepwalking through the party as though in trauma, and she had been depressed for at least a month before that.

At that time Meg still had words for what ailed her. "I'm afraid that this baby won't mean much, because I was given up by my birth mother," she said in a monotone when Ellen asked what was wrong.

At this point she still placed her feelings within herself. That is, she said "I" when describing her emotions. Later, "I" disappeared. Her apathy, contrasted with the rejoicing of everyone around her, was alarming.

"'Mean much,' *this* baby? Just look around you," Ellen pleaded. She became shrill, as though to animate Meg.

Dorothy's friends were honoring her first grandchild with striped sleepers, crib bumpers in a pattern of a towheaded kid in green overalls, a handmade sweater, and booties. Dorothy's aged mother had made a quilt with children in sunbonnets on it and mailed the quilt so it would reach Meg in advance of the birth. As Ellen and Meg folded the quilt into its box together, Meg shrugged in response, "I know."

Ellen knelt to gather wrapping paper and ribbon. Meg went to the laden dining room table for chicken salad and did not come back. Ellen saw that she had sat down alone. She looked resigned. Ellen felt even more uneasy.

Ellen and Will had adopted Meg at birth, but the adoption could not be finalized for several months because the birth mother retained the right to change her mind. Ellen recalled those months and remembered that she had gone into an agitated depression out of fear that Meg's mother would suddenly claim her. She particularly remembered the anguish of that first month of Meg's life. It filled Ellen with guilt to think that Meg might be so subdued and prone to depression because Ellen, her adoptive mother, was not fully available to her when she was born. Something had slipped. The mother-child bonding did not seal tight, and because of that, Meg and her soon-to-be-born child were at risk. Ellen could hardly face the thought that she had started a chain reaction all those years ago.

When Jane was born several weeks later, the delivery was difficult. Yet Meg rallied afterwards. Ellen spent the next day with her in her hospital room. The hours flew by, and they both watched the baby as she nursed and Meg patted her back to sleep. Jane yawned and made inquiring noises, and Meg would pick her up, check her diaper, and coo to her. To Ellen, being with Meg that day with the baby was life at its most sublime. She wrote of her happiness in her journal, believing that Meg's depression had passed. Even so, Ellen could not dismiss the unease she had felt over the past few months.

When Meg and the baby returned home, it became clear that the same issues that surrounded Meg's own birth were now gathering around this new child. Ellen had begun to think that adoption and cutting off were connected. Meg described a fear she could not shake, that someone would take the baby from her. Her mother urged Meg again, as she had since late in the pregnancy, to see a therapist, but Meg shrugged off the suggestion each time. Ellen tried to interpret Meg's fear in the light of Meg's own history. "But that was me!" Ellen told Meg. "I stole the baby, and that was you. I took the baby from your mother, and that baby was you. That must have made you terribly afraid, and somehow that old fear has come around again."

"But I was three days old then. This is something different," Meg countered.

"Couldn't it be a replay of my experience with you?" Ellen cried. "I was anxious for months right after we got you because I was afraid that I might lose you in that waiting period, and I think that hurt our connection, too. And things get so mixed up with mothers and babies that it may even be my fear from that time that you're responding to now. I told you the story, I know, and maybe you felt my anxiety then and are acting it out now."

Meg looked down and didn't answer this outpouring, a sign that she was emotionally removing herself.

"'Psychology garbage,' right?" Ellen asked rhetorically.

Meg looked away. She used to say, with spirit, "Get real," when Ellen would give psychological interpretations, but not now.

Ellen spoke quickly, to stop Meg from turning away altogether. "Or maybe you're living out what you thought your birth mother felt. You're living out your pity for her. In that scenario, you're her and I'm me."

"Now you've got about a million reasons," Meg said.

"Well, everything has layers."

"To you, not to normal people."

"Well, then, what is it?" Ellen asked. "It sounds like an adoption drama, and it looks like I play the witch."

That was during the short lucid period between them when the light flickered briefly. While the light was still on, Meg said, "I feel I could walk away from anything at any time. I just don't feel connected. I feel that someone is going to steal my baby." And she asked a lot of questions about her adoption. Meg told her mother that her childhood was unhappy because of Ellen's emphasis on achievement. Meg said that Ellen never wanted to speak to her on the phone and that her father did all the calling. She said that her mother only started to call her when she became pregnant because then at last "I had some worth to you." Meg was cold and angry, but flat. There was no passion in her anger as she told her mother off. Nevertheless, she had told her mother something real. Ellen asked whether she had failed Meg in any other way, and Meg said, suddenly, like a dutiful child, "I can't think of any other way now."

Ellen remembered another conversation. She and Meg spoke on the phone on a rainy afternoon late in the month after the baby was born. Meg was baking chicken and cooking vegetables. Ellen could imagine Meg's kitchen as they spoke, with its well-ordered countertops and immaculate stove. Everything in Meg's life was under control. Meg and her husband Roger were both intensely domestic: they painted, did repairs, and kept a vegetable garden. Together they were tireless, uncomplaining, and merged.

This was at the time when Meg was planning to go back to work at the magazine. She found it hard to think about leaving the baby. She wondered to Ellen whether it was because she had been adopted. Meg could not accept that the baby would be well enough cared for by anyone else. While every mother has the same worry, Ellen suspected that Meg had an additional one: that the baby-sitter would steal the baby. Meg also told Ellen that she felt "provisional," a word that echoed for a long time over the phone line and puzzled Ellen. Ellen asked about it. Meg answered that she had the feeling she herself might walk out at anytime.

"Is that why you don't make friends?" Ellen asked.

"It's like I'm waiting to see."

"You don't know where you're supposed to be?"

"I guess so."

Meg became more and more laconic as that conversation progressed. Ellen heard the apathy in her voice. Meg did not seem to care how anything came out. Her mother had to pull everything she wanted to know from her. Ellen felt like a prying psychologist, but she thought that if Meg could verbalize it, whatever it was, they might have a chance to revive their relationship. If Meg could recognize feelings and bring them into the open instead of burying them, she might begin to reflect on her emotions and ask herself, "Why?"

Ellen wanted to have a party for friends and family to meet

her first grandchild, but Meg said that she did not feel "connect-ed" to friends and family. Her original feeling of being discon-nected from her mother was spreading to other people in her mother's life.

On Mother's Day, Meg made a rare visit to her parents' house. She was angry, yet forthright; she again told Ellen that she had had an unhappy childhood. She asked more questions about her adoption.

Ellen asked Meg how she had failed her.

No, Meg could not put words to it. She said she did not want to talk about it anymore, yet she kept repeating how miser-able she had been growing up.

Ellen felt awful. Her anxiety was relieved only when Meg asked her questions she could answer. That meant Meg was still there and still talking. Yet Ellen knew in her heart that Meg was in the process of shutting down and moving away from her, if she was not already gone. Ellen had not guessed that Meg's child-hood was unhappy. What Meg said did not fit Ellen's memories. To Ellen, Meg's withdrawal made no sense.

Meg's mood at this time seemed to be less a depression than a blankness. Meg continued to do everything superlatively well: she was dexterous, she saw the connection between parts of things instantly, and she had a fine artistic sense. But she seemed to be performing her life like a brilliant sleepwalker. Moreover, once the process of estrangement was under way, there seemed to be no way for Ellen to stop it. Meg could not be aroused from her apathy. It was like watching over a sickbed when you cannot awaken the patient long enough to find out what the person needs. Even with someone there, Meg was isolated. She had removed herself from her family's lives. That was bad enough. Worse, she seemed unaware of herself and ungrounded in her own life.

Despite this, Meg was most attentive to the baby, diligent but low-keyed, without any show of joy. To Ellen, Meg's passivity was scary. Meg's husband, Roger, had always been staid and efficient, always on hand and responsive to Meg's orders. Effortlessly self-sufficient as a couple, they seemed to need no one. It was awkward enough at the best of times to be with these comfortable isolates, but Ellen felt that her presence now only deepened the silence between them. She felt even more tentative when she was with them because of Meg's lack of connection and her expressed fear that someone (whom Ellen thought must be herself) would steal the baby. After that Mother's Day, Meg was even more removed and harder to reach.

Nevertheless, Ellen tried to see Meg as often as she would allow. Later, amid the emotional wreckage, there was one scene that seemed like an epiphany. One late golden afternoon while Ellen was visiting, Jane awoke from her nap in the playroom and Ellen saw that the child was wearing a little red playsuit she had given her. Meg was blowing bubbles all around her. A good sign? Ellen asked herself. Though Ellen's and Meg's relationship had deteriorated, in that moment Ellen felt again the restful calm in her daughter that had always drawn her to Meg in a roomful of people. These days, however, Ellen was more careful, waiting to be told how to help, waiting to be offered the baby to hold. When Jane was five weeks old and giving them a few lopsided smiles, Ellen sang "The Fox" and "The Big Rock Candy Mountain" to her, with Meg's permission. They were songs that Meg had liked as a child, and Ellen hoped her daughter would join in and that this strange ordeal could end. Yet, as her mother sang, Meg busied herself with folding the baby's undershirts, as though she had not heard.

With some exceptions in their rare occasions together, Meg did not seem to mind her mother's physical presence. At the end of a rare visit on a beautiful day when they had been outdoors, Ellen heard Meg say with surprise, partially to herself but partly also to her mother because Ellen was only a few feet from her, "That wasn't so bad." In that way, too, Meg was like a sleepwalker. She did not question herself about her actions but only commented on them afterward. Another time, when her parents had begged to visit and Meg grudgingly acquiesced, Jane got fussy. "Now see what you've done!" she admonished Ellen.

"I didn't do it!" Ellen protested.

"I know it," Meg replied, with utter calmness, her old self speaking. But she could not hold onto those glimpses of another part of herself or another part of her mother. When Ellen kissed Meg goodbye and hugged her, it was like embracing a post. There was no response: Meg looked straight ahead. What her mother felt from her as Meg backed away was not anger. It was a kind of blankness.

Estrangement

The process of estrangement between Ellen and Meg was strange in itself: Meg seemed to envision having two mothers in one. The physical mother was a blank, a semblance and a shell. The other mother was someone she feared. The mother who was an effigy saved her from feeling afraid of the monster mother. As an effigy, Ellen felt that she was a person who came and went and was forgotten. She had no history of her own, nor did she and Meg share a past. She learned quickly not to speak of herself, because Meg could not relate to anything about her. Her mother's presence in her house was something to prepare for and also to disregard. Meg cooked wonderful meals when Ellen came, but she became silent during them, bland and emptied of thought. When she and Ellen were in a room together with just the baby, they did not marvel over her. That would have been unseemly in the stiff atmosphere. It would have been presumptuous, too. Making much of her as though Ellen had something to be proud of would indicate there was a connection between the baby and this woman.

The Cocoon Defense

All voluntary cutoffs are in a condition of psychic isolation before they cut off; all are defending against connection; all need to remain hidden, unfound, unrelated. Psychologists remind us that unrelatedness is the message and the medium. They tell us that there are various ways to recognize psychic isolation, including compliance versus active interest in another and the quality of a person's speech and silences. There is also the "feel of it." That is, when one feels isolated and alone in the presence of someone with this defense, it is often because one is indeed being isolated by the other person. In other words, an isolated person reveals his condition by isolating others!

For example, unrelated persons often show a fake front. They are the people who go along for the ride and never put in their two cents' worth. They are willing and docile. Their replies are compliant ("uh-huh, uh-huh"), but they show no warmth or interest in the other person. Essentially, they relate only to themselves and so do not initiate relationships on their own. Forced to "relate," the person passively awaits signals from the outside world on how to behave and then delivers a performance to order. For that reason all interaction feels hollow, even when the response is right and seems sincere.

When one person speaks to another or, let us say, asks something of the other, there is communication about the state of relatedness between the two people as well as the message itself. The feeling between the two is conveyed by tone of voice and body language. If the speaker is trying to communicate something real, the tone of voice alone will ask for a response. It will convey a real need and a genuine attempt to reach the other person. On the other hand, when words are empty of feeling, the absence of need is communicated. The subliminal message is, "I will not let you in. I will not hear you."

Unrelatedness is the medium of psychic isolation. It is a

powerful refusal, a way to say "I won't let you in" without words. It is a way to defend against communication without being noticed except as someone who is often quiet. Unrelatedness is not a passive defense although it may fool us into thinking so. It is an active strategy, just as a protester who goes limp when a police officer tries to arrest him is actively using inactivity as a strategy. Unrelatedness is an active strategy when it impels a person who has cut off to leave home. It is an *active* two-person defense that is always directed against someone else.

All defenses are unconscious, but when the defense is unrelatedness the person against whom the defense is directed knows that the feelings have been induced in him from without. He has a conscious reaction. The unrelated person, on the other hand, is acting naturally and is unaware of having any effect on another person. For example, Meg was not necessarily aware that her behavior had an effect on Ellen.

In ordinary passive aggression, the speaker is usually aware when he uses the wrong name or keeps someone waiting. Meg's defense was different. For instance, she continued to call her mother-in-law Dots, although Meg knew that Dorothy is what her mother-in-law preferred. Meg could not relate to another's wishes, because to do so felt too much as though she was giving up control.

A lack of connection and a refusal to speak are parts of an active defense against relating. They support the illusion of being complete in oneself, for isolation is a defense against needing anyone, and relating undermines the illusion. As a child Meg was shy but responsive and witty. She enjoyed joking and teasing. She was actively involved in give and take with others. Now, a response of any kind felt like submission. The defense was directed against her mother, but it was clear even at the baby shower, when she withdrew from the other guests and barely responded when spoken to, that it had spread to other people.

To give up major relationships, a person has to give up minor ones as well. The person must really believe that he or she needs no one. Otherwise, they will always be faced with temptation. The cocoon is the only safe place to live. Old familiar places must be avoided. Meg came to her parents' house only once after Mother's Day and that was to clean out her things. It would have been too evocative for her to come again as she had lived in their home for twenty years, and she avoided the knowledge. Meanwhile, the part of Ellen that to Meg had always been unpleasant grew larger and larger in Meg's consciousness until it dominated her view. With time and estrangement, this view became phobic. Meg's need to view Ellen that way always came between her and her mother's actual qualities, both good and bad.

In the early days of their estrangement, Ellen felt it was a struggle for Meg to forget the first twenty years of her life, as when Meg had talked so frankly about a lack of communication between them. With distance and time, however, forgetting became more effective, and Meg seemed to have truly forgotten the old connection. It was an unconscious process with a preconscious warning system: say no to anything connected in any way to those bad old days.

The Culminating Incident

For a year and a half Ellen and Will tried to see Meg. She resisted their attempts politely but evasively, and each visit felt like an extortion. They tried to see her once a month, or every six weeks, for short visits, but most attempts were rebuffed. The time stretched between visits, and most arrangements required several preparatory phone calls, which lengthened the time further. Although Ellen rehearsed keeping calm beforehand, she was often shrill and pleading when she phoned, or sarcastic: "This is the wrong mother again." After she had spoken, whether calmly or hysterically, there was usually an edgy silence and then a brief explanation from Meg of why whatever Ellen proposed was not possible. Her mother would offer another date and ask Meg to think about it and let them know her answer, but that did not work. Meg never initiated a return call, so Ellen would have to phone her again. Once Meg did make a date, however, she usually kept it.

No matter what the outcome of the phone call, Ellen would try to label what was happening and put a frame around it by saying, "No matter what you do, I will never cut off from you." What was happening, of course, was that Meg had already cut off from her mother, the "designated" cutoff. She seems to have extended the cutoff to her father Will and her brother David without particularly targeting them. Her parents were hanging in, and so the initiative always came from their side. In her heart, Ellen knew that Meg had cut off, but did not want to know because she had no choice but to try to get her back. She was stuck between denial and anger. As in any loss, there were levels and stages of acceptance and denial, and for a while Ellen careened crazily between them.

A deeper realization finally pervaded Ellen's dreams. When Jane was about one and a half years old, Ellen awoke from a nightmare in which Will and she were crying, mourning their lost daughter. The scene in the nightmare ended there but was prophetic.

Only a week later they went to see Meg, Roger, and the baby. It was on a Sunday in October just before the presidential election of 1988. The house and grounds were in perfect order as usual. The surrounding town looked like a calendar illustration, with the autumn leaves, dappled hillsides, and an occasional red barn. They all went to a local restaurant and started talking politics. Roger was an articulate Libertarian. He said that Dukakis was arrogant with "that Boston-Harvard crowd behind him" and added that, although Bush might be mediocre, he did not mind four years of mediocrity or intrusion in the bedroom as long as no one interfered with free trade. He had grown up in Princeton, which he scorned for its liberal bias. He was suspicious of anyone resembling an academic. Meg added that both major parties had too many regulations about licensing child care and said she, too, would vote Libertarian. Outwardly the young couple were talking politics but their body language and tone of voice made what they said sound to Ellen as a metaphor for leaving the family.

Meg is dark, pretty, and extremely tall. Her glossy black hair was worn in a single long braid that day. Ellen could not help thinking that Meg had consolidated her position and was getting stronger and more alive the longer she was apart from her mother. Ellen herself was feeling especially dead and depressed from the mourning dream she'd had the week before. It had seemed so true that she could barely speak to Meg until they got to the restaurant. Now she felt inert, as though Meg had finally placed her deadness into Ellen and taken on a new life herself. Meg was bright and smiling for the first time in eighteen months. They had reversed their emotional responses.

Back at Meg's house, Ellen asked Meg about going into family therapy. "I want to do it," Ellen explained, "because you are close to your new family, and pushed your old family out, and because I don't accept that I am a villain." She told Meg that she had found a therapist who practiced in a town halfway between them, about an hour's drive for each of them. "We could see him once a month for as long as it takes," Ellen pleaded.

Meg said she would think about it, but what about her brother David? David was three years younger, also adopted, and there were bound to be issues involving him. Yet David lived three thousand miles away! Ellen explained that as the trouble was between Meg and herself she thought they should start right away and work out logistics with David later. Meg's insistence on David's participation struck Ellen as an evasion.

If that was the case, Meg asked, then why was her father going? She said that her parents seemed to be getting along better. Ellen told Meg that was because Will was getting good therapy. Meg quipped, "Does he get a report card?" It was a hostile question but a sign of the new life Meg was showing that day. Meg asked her father what he thought.

He told her, "I find that putting things off works only in the short term."

Meg did not want to talk about family therapy anymore, she said, and so they switched to discussing the idea of a family get-together in January. Meg seemed most amenable.

Trouble started when Ellen told Meg that she would like to be sure that they celebrated Jane's birthday, whether at her house or theirs. Meg said that depended on what Ellen meant by "celebrate."

Ellen replied, "Cake and ice cream." Ellen sensed by Meg's tone and manner that she was feeling angry about all the people she did not feel connected to.

Ellen said it was already clear to them that Meg had not wanted to invite Will and her mother at all in the past year. The one call that she had made to her mother in eighteen months was to disinvite her grandfather, whom Ellen had asked her to invite. Meg said that Ellen was trying to control her. Meg became angrier and began commenting about how "mean" she must be, and "I suppose I'm mean to the baby and Roger too, mean about everything."

Ellen replied, "No. You're just mean and hateful to me."

At that point Meg got up, pointed to the door, and said, "Get out! Get out!" and then physically got behind Ellen and pushed her out of the house. Roger and Will both looked hangdog but did nothing. When Will got no other signal from Meg, he left too.

The Official Cutoff

Once the cutoff was "official," two things saved Ellen from complete despair. First, she refused the designation of terminal cutoff by writing to Meg, "I will never cut off from you no matter what you do." Writing this gave Ellen some relief, even though Meg did not reply. Next, Ellen tried in every way she could to figure out what had gone wrong between them and how to get her daughter back. As honestly as she could, she looked back over their history together. She reviewed their everyday family life, her own shortcomings as a mother, particularly in the early years, the kind of people they all were, and relations among Will, Meg, David, and herself. Ellen concluded that Meg's quarrel seemed to be with her.

Having studied psychology, Ellen was painfully aware of the role of family history in this cutoff. There had been a cluster of strange cutoffs in her own family. Two brothers on Ellen's father's side and a brother and a sister on her mother's side, all from the same village in Ireland, had emigrated to the United States but no one had been able to find them once they got here. Her father's older brother Eamon designated his father as the one he was fleeing from after they had a violent fight, but no one in the family knew why the other three had cut off. Perhaps Eamon influenced them, and they formed their own enclave in America. Perhaps when they left they felt pushed out of the nest (the village was poor) and wanted no part of the families that had not wanted them. In any case, the investment was gone.

This last was Meg's attitude toward her brother David. She just stopped investing in him. Ellen thought that a cutoff by association might be less poisonous and hoped that she could work for a rapprochement between brother and sister that might take place after her death, if Meg's cutoff from her was indeed final.

However, Ellen couldn't accept this fate. She remembered carrying Meg on her hip as a baby, her pleasure in Meg's placid nature, and how early Meg walked and talked. They called her the Easy Baby. Sometimes Ellen cried out, "Face, face!" Meg's face was so beautiful as a small child, round and fair with wispy curling hair around it. Photographs from that time did not help, Ellen found, because they all seemed to have been taken at happy times: in the Caribbean, on the beach at Wellfleet, on horses out west, with dogs and cats at home, or among the happy dishevelment of wrappings near the Christmas tree.

In one of the pictures Meg had fallen asleep on the couch when she was about six years old. She was wearing an old-fashioned mobcap and matching nightgown. Behind her the bookshelves were crammed, and a picture book lay face down on the floor. In other pictures, Will played the piano while Meg played the flute. In another photo taken at a birthday party Meg was sitting at the head of the table in front of the cake, laughing. In still another photo taken at another birthday party on Cape Cod, old wooden chairs had been dragged onto the scraggly lawn around their neighbor's sculptures, a dozen kids were milling around, and one boy had a guitar. It looked as though it might have been fun, Meg's childhood, but Ellen thought, she might be editing these memories.

Family photographs reflect the moment, but the photos one saves also document a family myth. "Perhaps we unconsciously edit the scenes we record, preserving the illusion we want to achieve, for there is no foreshadowing in the photographs of the dark feelings that were to come," she said.

Searching for an explanation, Ellen often went back to her fear of losing Meg to her birth mother, who had given Meg up at birth. Still, the woman had had six months to change her mind. During that time, the worry never left Ellen. Ellen remembers that there was a fire in the neighborhood one evening at dusk when Meg was about a month old. She and Will went out to see it. The street was alight with fire and the air was clogged with smoke. The streetlights were out, and, in the shadow of fire and haze, the neighbors she was talking to, Dori and Franz, looked like apparitions. They must have seen the same thing in her. "You look like you've seen a ghost," Dori said.

The fragile web between mother and child may be torn by a mother's anxiety, since the child can feel her anxiety only as a danger to itself. "A woman who ordinarily would be a 'good-enough mother,'" as D. W. Winnicott puts it, "may have suffered a severe blow in life at the time of the birth . . . and this may be sufficient to disturb her mothering of a particular infant." The trouble between Meg and Ellen feels to Ellen like a deep primitive connection gone wrong at an early stage. She wonders whether living in fear as she had during those first six months of Meg's life may have disrupted their bond. She wonders whether that loopy, dreamy space between mother and infant was lost in those early months, that space jointly created in which the infant "begins to be," as Winnicott says. He calls it potential space, and in this space the dialogue between the mother and child starts.

From this early dialogue the child creates its world. She begins to perceive the relation between reality and fantasy, of the me and not-me. Emotions are tried on and serve as signals between the child and its mother, first, and later, as signals of the child to himself. The mother endorses the child's feelings, whatever they may be, and shows her approval in her behavior.

Ellen could not deny to herself that adoption might have had a great deal to do with Meg's feelings. Ellen knew something about adoption from her studies. The cutoff from biological parents which the child endures, the complicated development issues for adoptees, and the double-bound and alienated adoptive parents all help to explain the high rate of failure of adoptions better than either nature or nurture, alone or together. Ellen knew that this did not mean that adoption is doomed to failure, only that the splits, cutoffs, and double binds, often hidden from view in adoption, that prevented connection must be exposed to light. A deep connection to the adoption process was, she knew, the best defense. A healthy outcome would depend on an awareness of its pitfalls.

The closest Ellen can come to understanding how she might have failed Meg is by looking at how she herself responds when she comes flat up against reality. Ellen had an odd insight into that the previous summer at the lake when she suddenly caught herself immersed in the lives of a family having a day's outing at the beach. The middle child, a tall, sturdy girl of about eight, ran in and out of the water, while her two-year-old brother patted the wet sand vigorously with his trowel. The oldest child, a bony boy of ten or so, wore a T-shirt and cap, and his head wobbled on his thin neck. He held his mother's hand and approached the water with alarm, taking tiny steps. The mother was infinitely patient and attentive to him but she seemed relaxed and aware of the other children's activities, too. The father floated into the shore from swimming far out and gave the two-year-old a hand with his sandpile.

Ellen observed her own anxiety rise. In her mind there was no separation between her and this family. What terrible catastrophe had overtaken the oldest child, and how could the parents be so calm about it? For a minute she felt as though she were the mother of all three children. If I were that mother, Ellen thought, my grief for the oldest child would be so great that it would be a wonder to me that the younger two were so sturdy and fine. As she let her imagination take flight, Ellen realized that in the mother's place she certainly would have no time for anything except her worry over the older boy. As the mother of the disabled child, Ellen would throw herself into her grief so thoroughly that there would be no room for any more devastation or any awful surprises in her life. She would feel that the tragedy had occurred because she had not been alert enough to watch that the pain of the boy's leukemia (or autism) had eluded her.

One must be alarmed in advance! She had dreaded the birth mother's arrival every minute of the waiting period until

Meg was legally theirs. Otherwise, one must steep oneself in pain after the disaster occurs, as Ellen had at the lake on behalf of the calm couple who failed to be anxious. She had to care because they failed to care. Why did they fail in keeping their oldest child safe from harm? Because, she believed, they were too engaged in the moment, in living with their children.

The most extreme case of Ellen's kind of preparation for disaster had also occurred in the life of another client of mine, Gayle Roberts. Mrs. Roberts had been rather reclusive while her children were growing up and began leaving the house less and less. About eight years ago she had an ordinary eye examination. The doctor noticed something that made him suspicious and referred her to a specialist. Instead of going to the specialist's office to make an appointment, she went home and got ready to die. After that day she never left the house again. At first she confined herself to a chair in the bedroom. Later, she turned her bedroom into a hospital room with a hospital bed in which she lay day and night, ready for death to come.

Ellen wonders now whether she was suffering in advance of losing Meg, grieving beforehand for a loss that would be unbearable to her should it happen at all, and, as it was for Mrs. Roberts, be even more devastating were she unprepared. What if she had not been fully available to Meg as a baby, because she was preparing for her loss? Maybe she had failed to give herself to her daughter completely in the first six months, so that an inchoate resentment had grown in Meg from the start? Was she attuned to her? Did she really know her? Did she notice nuances of feeling in her? Christopher Bollas, a psychoanalyst, says, "Although her mothering may be very disturbed for a period of time [a mother] might recover to become a good-enough mother." Ellen agonizes about whether she ever became a good-enough mother.

The Child Who Made Herself a Ghost

The night that Meg threw her mother out bodily, Ellen remembers coming home and wandering about the lawn in the dark, silly with shock, grinning incongruously. When she finally went inside there was a news item on television about a family that was trying to reclaim their son from a cult. What she remembers best from that day, she says, is the hard white face of the young Moonie as he pushed his frantic parents out the door of the cult house.

Ellen felt as those parents must have. Meg was not dead nor was she in some country far away. She was living with her husband and daughter two hundred miles away, but she had made herself dead to her parents. "Whenever she came back to our house," Ellen says, "it was not as a daughter but to empty the house of all its associations of the daughter she used to be." Meg came one day and swept all her belongings into shopping bags. Her movements were vigorous and final. She swept the past from the room she grew up in, emptying it of herself. She threw out piles of school notebooks and dog-eared favorite storybooks and old skirts and sweaters that she used to wear around the house when she stayed with her parents. She took all her baby pictures. She pulled out her old English compositions and threw them away. One of these, written when she was about eight, was about a little girl who crawls through a tunnel to make a connection with her real family, a group of Martians. They are odd but nice, and she would like to stay with them. But she has to crawl back to the family she is living with, the story goes, or they will get mad at her. Meg probably showed Ellen that composition when she was a child, and Ellen now says, reflecting, "I must have been willfully blind not to see the message."

When Meg threw her parents out of her house, she was defending her new identity as someone who was her own mother and had no living relatives. When Ellen said, "Don't forget me, don't forget your father, don't forget that we are related to you and the baby," Meg had already shut out her parents and was settling into her fantasy. Since Ellen was threatening the premise of the fantasy, Ellen had to go. From Meg's standpoint, who was "mother," anyway? A mother was no longer in Meg's life, so Ellen must have seemed like an importuning stranger threatening her security and well-being. As it seemed to her then, Meg was merely protecting herself.

But how had her mother of twenty-seven years disappeared from Meg's inner thoughts and life?

Meg Dissociates and Becomes Her Own Mother

Ellen's disappearance from Meg's psychic life seems to have happened through dissociation. In a recent issue of the *Harvard Mental Health Letter* on dissociation, such a condition is described this way:

"Attention is focused, context is lost, and unwanted or unneeded feelings are excluded from awareness as in hypnotic trances. Some common results are detachment from the self or surroundings and partial or total amnesia."

An emotional numbing occurs. The dissociated does not want to talk or think about the trauma and may find that more and more areas of her life will not bear the pain of examination. This emotional numbing is familiar from ordinary experience, as when, for example, we feel numb after trauma or turn away from a gruesome traffic accident. The process of dissociation in some cases can be quite pleasant, as in yoga or hypnosis when you sink down into yourself. True dissociation is like permanent self-hypnosis in which the person does not emerge from the trance. Connections, continuity, and consistency are lost, and the person's sense of identity changes. The *Mental Health Letter* goes on to tell us: "Groups of memories, feelings, and perceptions are relegated to separate compartments or buried in oblivion from which they may suddenly emerge."

As far as Ellen could tell, the dissociation seemed to be complete for Meg, who had survived the crisis of identity that had become so acute during her pregnancy. In stages from then on she had reorganized her inner self to meet the crisis, and through dissociation and displacement she had completed the cutoff. Meg had gone from depression to apathy to putting the problem outside herself. Her paranoia became a defense against her depression. And this defense held: Will and Ellen represented the bad past, they deserved to be banished, and that was that. Meg felt she was defending her child. Meg's solution was to be protective of her baby, for she could not give herself to her child if she were depressed. However, she could give of herself if the past disappeared, was "excluded from awareness," or was projected elsewhere with all the uncomfortable feelings connected with it. It all made emotional sense to Ellen, although it was very hurtful to her.

Meg consolidated this position in the months after Jane's birth by becoming a mother to herself. She thus resolved the problem which had overwhelmed her over her own birth. She appeared to feel: one woman had given her away; the other woman stole her. A plague on both of them. Becoming her own mother was an unconscious solution, a psychological fit, and day to day Meg's own tremendous competence made it work and reinforced it. She was quick, efficient and frugal, and rarely needed to call on anyone for help. Her husband Roger provided another psychological fit, with his tremendous appetite for work and his need to be hidden away.

Meg had no family, it seemed to her, so she had made her own. The feeling of being uprooted, unclaimed, free-floating, and a member of the wrong family, as the Martian composition she had left behind had reminded Ellen, was with Meg from the time she was a child. She had felt provisional, as she called it, for a long time before she cut off, and cutting off was the only way to erase the tormenting question of origin. During her pregnancy with Jane and for three or four months afterward, Meg was in transition, at the mercy of two families: one that she did not want, and another that had failed to claim her. Both reminded her of her pain. She and Roger went on to create their own family rapidly. During the next few years she had another child and she was free from depression. By this time she was under the belljar, and her parents were outside her consciousness. She was not using words like *provisional* anymore, nor was she voicing the fear that someone would steal her baby. She was not even saying "I" anymore, for at that point everything had become black and white, and she was no longer observing her own behavior.

Meg kept distance between herself and her parents because their presence would raise the question of who they were to her. She had solved that question by banishing them from both her house and her memory. Thus Meg was able to ignore them without rancor and turned cruel only when Ellen and Will made a claim for connection. Then Meg protected her children, whom, she felt unconsciously, they would steal. When Ellen verbalized this unconscious feeling, trying to make the idea conscious for Meg, Meg ignored her. Indeed, Ellen's "bleating" must have felt outlandish to Meg, for she had dissociated the relationship completely, and so really did not know what in the world this woman was going on about.

Yet, how can one forget a mother and father of twenty-seven years, simply forget years of daily living, good or bad, the coloration their presence gave to her life? Gone, all gone. Who would believe that amnesia could be so thorough? Yet if "groups of memories, feelings, and perceptions are relegated to separate compartments or buried in oblivion from which they may suddenly emerge," does that not mean that there may be some way to retrieve them and bring the memories back?

It was this hope which had brought Ellen to me. And as I looked into other situations of cutting off, I searched for methods by which she, myself, and others who had severed relationships, could reconnect.

3

CUTOFFS
IN THE FAMILY

Particular ways for dealing with family problems are passed from one generation to the next. Often, the major problems of the current family will also have occurred in previous generations. Symptomatic patterns such as alcoholism, child abuse, somaticizing, violence, and suicide tend to exist in several generations.

In dealing with such crises a family often uses whatever mechanisms it has inherited from previous generations. These regulate its internal processes and, because they are part of the family's history, these mechanisms feel natural, powerful, and right.

Thus, once families of one generation have begun the phenomenon of cutting off as a way of dealing with pain, subsequent generations also tend to use banishment to deal with theirs. Death, divorce, adoption, and emigration are often occasions for cutting off.

Any family may also cut off a member when the family feels shamed or disgraced. Among the many issues that precipitate such cutoffs are alcoholism, a change in religion, AIDS, a child joining a cult, criminality, drugs, a grown child who fails to meet family standards, homosexuality, illegitimacy, mixed marriage, psychosis, retardation, and scandal.

Whatever the reasons for it occurring, cutting off has a pathological afterlife within the family. When the one who is gone, even through death, is not spoken about out of pain, guilt, or shame, over time she or he becomes a nonperson. When the strongest family member takes this stance, even silently, the others readily follow suit. Silence stills their pain, guilt, or shame, and so the dissociation is self-reinforcing. Moreover, if this is the family mechanism for dealing with emotional pain, to the others it feels just right.

MY MOTHER

My mother cut off from me during the last twelve years of her life. She summoned me briefly in 1990, a year before she died, but three months later dismissed me again and died still cut off from me. She and my brother sent me a certified letter telling me not to annoy her anymore, and she died shortly after in a nursing home located close to him.

She had cut off many times before. Sometimes I made a clumsy effort at retrieval, but my efforts failed. She was more expert at losing than I was at finding. After my father's death, she cut off from his family; later she cut off from her sister, me, and two of her grandchildren by inadvertence (they were mine), and a third by fiat (my brother's child; my brother had cut off from him.)

The process, however, began earlier, when my mother's father left his family in America. After a short stay in Poland to visit the children of his first marriage, he was caught in the First World War and was not able to return for ten years. (An irony of this history is that, in going back home, my grandfather was trying not to cut off from his earlier family.) My mother was eight when her father left. She felt abandoned; his loss was both devastating and humiliating for her. She felt foolish. She had counted on her father's love and could no longer do so. For her, this was the prototypical affront and established a lifelong pattern of leaving people before they left her.

Her life was a series of these little leavings. My mother cut off from aunts and uncles and cousins on her side of the family over some offense. She even cut off on telephone conversations as a matter of habit, hanging up before the other person had finished speaking. If she sometimes grew sentimental about an older living relative, it was only in order to hold on to a good image as she never went to see the person. She liked people to woo her; then she quarreled with them and cut them off. I suspect that this is what she had always wanted to do but never could do with the father who had disappeared for so long. She experienced absence and even death as a deliberate slight, and could not distinguish between them. Thirty years after my father's death she said bitterly, "He had to go and leave me!" To her, death by cancer was an act of spite.

Her words must have been meant for my grandfather as well; her father may have gone to visit his first family suddenly. My mother's abrupt behavior often seemed to be a reenactment of his leaving, the difference being that she took charge; she won; she left first; she was in control of leaving. She would do the leaving first—before the other person could leave her—and she made sure that the other person knew it. It certainly was imperative for her to cut off; it was an overriding impulse, she revenged herself wherever she could.

Once, when I was driving the car, she jumped out at a stoplight in the middle of nowhere, although nothing special had happened. "I'm not riding with you!" she said. Much as an abused child in turn abuses her own child, my mother cut off in blind retaliation for having been cut off by her father.

For more than a decade at the end of her life, she cut off from me. About five years before she died, I dreamed that our cat, Charlotte, was sitting in the back seat of our car. Charlotte is a cantankerous old calico, a grim loner who was rescued from a garbage can in the ghetto as a kitten and as an old cat still keeps to herself. At one time, she and my mother kept about the same wary distance from me—Charlotte, in the garden, sometimes coming in for meals; my mother fifteen blocks away, doing the same. In the dream I said to my husband, "It's too bad that Charlotte is so alone. It's too bad that she has no daughter." My husband said, "She has a daughter."

The dream admonished me and left me in its power. Still held by it on the following morning, I called my mother. She picked up on the third ring and seemed to know who I was right away. There was actually something welcoming in her voice. In kind of a mock grumble she asked why I was calling her. I told her that I was calling to say that I looked in the mirror and saw that I looked like her. I said that she did not have to forgive me but that I forgave her. She began her plaint slowly: what had she ever done to forgive? There was no wrong on her side. I had let her rot for years. She repeated a couple of times that I had ruined her old age. She was gathering steam. "All these Thanksgivings I lay alone, and you invite everyone but me." She began to scream, but I was prepared, telling her:

"Hold on and I'll be right over."

She yelled, "Over my dead body" and hung up. I went to see her anyway, and she screamed the same words through the door. Out in the hall, between rat-a-tats on the door, I tried to persuade her to let me in. This created some interest from her neighbors, but not from her, and after a while I went home.

About five years later, several months before she died, she left the same two messages on my machine one Sunday. "Call Mother." I called about 10:30 in the evening, wondering whether something was wrong. She said that she was all right, that she had "shopped and lived alone" even though she was ninety. I asked whether I could come to see her the next morning. She answered: "Whatever"—like a hip kid—and hung up. I could hardly believe that she had called me. It reminded me of something that had happened years earlier. My mother had not spoken to her sister in nine years. Then, one day at a funeral, Mother tapped her on the shoulder and said, "Hello, stupid." I wondered how long they spoke after that, before Mom cut her sister off again and for good.

My own reconciliation turned out to last only a little more than three months. I saw or spoke to her every day from September to early January, an unexpected bonus for one who has been cut off, a chance for some kind of closure. That first morning, when I got to the eighteenth floor, the door was open for me, and my mother was hovering nearby. She said, "You've gone gray." Then she was momentarily disoriented and asked me whether I had any children but remembered right away that I did. I had brought flowers, and she fussed around until she found a tall pickle jar for them. She fumbled to clean the countertop—she had been eating some dry toast when I came—and to open the balcony door for air. The blinds were twisted, and she allowed me to adjust them.

She was thin, painfully thin, and wore a pretty dress with a flowered print. It suited her. I thought I remembered it from years earlier. She also had several rayon shifts in the closet that I recognized. She wore dainty black pumps and stockings. Little came into that house; nothing ever left it. Her hair was still a reddish color, and she wore a braid down the back. When we went out she would tuck the braid under her blue sun hat with a jaunty motion, looking in the mirror as she did so.

We sat down in musty sunlight beneath an oblong mirror with a chipped frame. Time closed over, nothing at all had changed in the thirty years she had lived in that apartment that I could see. I remembered the same dusty pictures in the gray cardboard frames of forty-five years ago: my grandmother with her severe eyes and beautiful turned-up nose, her hair drawn into a bun, her skin pale; my mother as a young woman; my mother with the two of us as children, all of us looking fresh and clean with straight parts in our hair. There were some very old letters and my birthday card to her on her ninetieth birthday. She spoke of the world from her own point of view, as she had always done, but events were foreshortened, and people narrowed down to a characteristic or two.

What was remarkable to me was that at ninety she was not appreciably different from the way she had been in her seventies. Extreme old age seemed to have made only a few devastating inroads on her personality. Emotional foreshortening, for example, was a lifelong habit, a product of the way she viewed the world—at least from the time she was middle-aged. For example, during those three months when I visited her, she often reminisced in a condensed fashion, and some kind of doubt and guilt played about the edges of what she was saying. She would begin, "I made some mistakes," or "I made some little mistakes." I, of course, hoping for rapprochement, wanted to believe that she was about to talk about us. "Who doesn't make some mistakes? Nobody's perfect," she would continue, and I listened harder: my time was coming. It surely was coming. But, then, it did not come.

Then she would introduce the essential topic: "I paid fifty-two dollars a month rent in Queens. That was a cute little apartment, but I didn't make a mistake moving here. I get a breeze from my porch. When I keep the door open, it's like being outside. This is a nice building. I've got everything right at hand." The words were almost the same ones she had used during the first years after she had bought the apartment. Then sometimes she giggled and ended on a note of triumph, "I came all the way up to the eighteenth floor. Who would have thought—a widow?" Sometimes her voice would trail away, or she would repeat the set piece more firmly but without the "mistakes" and with more breezes, ships, and tugboats in the harbor. Her worst epithets were *weak* and *foolish*, and even after thirty years, she was still afraid that in buying an apartment she had somehow been weak and foolish.

I had kissed her when I came in and said how glad I was that she had called me. She reminded me that I had been very cruel to her, letting her lie like a dog every year while I had this one and that one in for holiday dinners. It was easy for her to invoke me as evil, for she had recreated my life in her mind as one long gala; she had festooned it with fetes and revels—a strawberry tea, my older daughter had called it—from which I had excluded her. Feeling persecuted helped her to stay cut off, and so she projected onto me the role of excluder. Ignoring her remarks, I told her that I admired the way that she held out. In the end that was her monument: her sheer perversity. Her endurance was formidable; it defied the odds. She would not give in, not to me and not to herself or to any living creature.

After a while, when I pressed her about why she had gotten in touch with me if she felt that I had been so cruel to her, she said that since she was ninety and did not know how much time she had, she had decided to forgive me. She added that it was up to the mother to forgive. Then she told me about having a pain in her stomach, like a tightness. It might be "mental," she said. I thought she might be telling me that the tightness and the telephone calls were connected. In a little while, she talked herself out of the discomfort by insisting that the tightness must, finally, be mental. In this I saw how she coped with alarm, alone, stoically making light of her own fears. She may have talked herself out of asking for help many times before this one. Yet now she could not seem to keep from talking about this tightness that was, according to her, only mental, in this way indicating that she was worried. I asked her how I could help her with the tightness. She did not want me to take her to the doctor, and she did not want medicine. I asked her whether the tightness was from something she was feeling, something she wanted to say to me or someone else. "No." Was she missing her mother and father? She said that that was all over.

I asked if she missed her sister. She said yes, she did miss her sister. I reminded her that she had not seemed to want to have anything to do with her sister for many years. Why was that? I asked. She seemed to be thinking a little about the reason. Then she explained that her sister had thought that her own husband was better than my mother and her husband (although one husband had been dead for thirty years, another for fifty). She also said that my aunt had "said things" about her. I said that although people had told her that, it was not true, that my aunt had missed her sister in her later years. To this my mother said that they had been like "two little girls together." She had several stock pieties, said in lowered, mincing tones, and this was one of them, even when, in the next breath, she said more truly and savagely, as she had in the past, "Let her go on welfare." Then she said, with a catch in her voice, "I miss her more than I miss anyone." Those words sounded painfully true.

When my aunt had become sick a few years earlier, I had let my mother know, but she did not respond. When my aunt died, my mother came to the funeral and then to my house. She was especially scurrilous about her sister. I have since learned the reason for this behavior through my sessions with a paranoid patient whose father and brother lay dying at the same time in the same hospital.

My patient, Jennifer Nolan, was venomous over an incident involving her brother wanting a yogurt and her father wanting a window closed. Jennifer, it turned out, was furious that her father and brother had played "a dirty trick" on her by making her trek to the hospital when they knew they were going to die. "Do they bother to think about my feelings?" Jennifer said. "No," she replied to herself, "and I'm not going to let them get away with it and make a fool out of me. I'll leave first." She was stating my mother's case as well as her own: All outside events for such people are seen through a subjective prism, a perspective most apparent in times of crisis. Like Jennifer, my mother was furious that her sister and her husband "had to go and leave" her.

The morning of our reunion, I tried to tell my mother about my aunt's girlishness and charm one spring evening in the hospital toward the end of her life: how my aunt had dangled her legs over the end of the bed and joked, telling stories on herself. My mother was generous in her response to this story, saying that my aunt had loved me from the moment I was born. She also said that she was never jealous about it.

She then said that it was my brother who took care of her, and I said that I took care of her sister. I put a gloss on this exchange, implying—in this family famous for its meaningless suffering—that we had divided up the duties in the natural way of things.

She said how wonderful my brother had been to her, how sweet he always was, and how he continued to be sweeter. "He is very tender with me," she simpered. He takes care of all of her business now, she said. She told me that she was very successful and that she was very rich, but that although she could buy what-ever she might need, she did not want anything and did not need anything.

Splendid Isolation

Not needing anything was important to my mother's illu-sion of self-sufficiency, which is an illusion that sustains all cutoffs. The less the person cutting off needs any person, place, or thing, the greater is the triumph of her or his splendid isolation. A cutoff must live as though there were no one else in the world. My mother asked nothing from anyone, including my brother. He could visit if he chose to, but she would not ask him to come and never called him. If he did not come, that was fine too.

She was beyond all such needs, for her greatest glory was living "on empty." At the time of her death she had two sheets, three cracked cups, a few forks which may have been from my father's restaurant supply business of a half century before, and a bent pot for a coffeemaker. She grew gay and giddy and strong on self-denial in the service of the illusion of self-sufficiency: two sheets were enough; she boasted that there was a washing machine in her apartment building. If she did not wash clothes on Tuesday, she could wash them on Wednesday or another day; she was stronger for it because she had denied herself something. If the sheets didn't dry, "Big deal," she would say; "I don't take myself so seriously." She could and would sleep on the old couch instead of the bed if she had to, and that was another triumph. Like a cloistered nun, she became radiant from self-denial.

When I was younger, I tried to trick her out of self-denial by inviting her to dinner every Sunday. She liked to walk, and it was a pleasant walk to my house. But as it was dark by the time dinner was over, she had to pay for a taxi to go home. If I drove her home, I would have lost my parking space. I reasoned that her family life would make the trade-off worth it to her, especially since I gave her food to take home, but it did not.

I misjudged her altogether. The taxi rankled her because it cost money. She wound up the loser every week. On her own, dinner would not be so fancy-schmancy, and the taxi emptied her of her widow's mite. She felt that I was trying to take control of her life, too, by ordering that cab every week. It put her into a rage. Finally, she just stopped coming. If there was emptying to do, she would do it in her own way and at her own pace.

I think now that I should have driven her home without a fuss instead of trying to impose reciprocity on her. Taking a cab humiliated her, and she turned me into her persecutor. On my side, I gained a kind of martyred self-aggrandizement, but the situation could only deteriorate as we both continued to play out our roles.

When my mother was about sixty, her life was about filling and emptying herself in proper measure. Later, emptying became an end it itself. It was safe and more congruent with splendid isolation because the emptying process could be entirely under one's own control. When I tried to put the filling and emptying under my control by having her take a taxi home after Sunday dinner, I lost her. She trashed anything I gave her during that time, as she was still smarting from the taxi humiliation and others like it, and from my subliminal demand that she see me as "good," which she would not do. She cut me off shortly thereafter.

I remember taking her to a restaurant noted for bountiful and varied fresh bread. She took home the whole basket of it from our table and laughed at my embarrassment. Then she warned me, "I'm going to teach you to leave me alone," and she meant it, for I had threatened her whole psychic economy. I had witnessed her need for something—the bread—and that was an unforgivable humiliation, proving that I was one of those busybodies who make fools out of other people if you let them. Her fear was of engulfment or merger, that the other person would control or dominate her mind. She complained that I had a need to show her that I was wealthy, a Mrs. Rockefeller, by taking her to a restaurant when she had never asked me or anyone else to take her to a restaurant. She didn't need it; she didn't want to go. "I never went to the movies once in twenty years, and it's right across the street, not like those stupid widows in my house that have to go all the time, and two together."

Her greatest pride was knowing how to deny herself. It was clear that the worst part of her humiliation was that I might not know how good she was at it. Later, I came to realize that her greed at the restaurant that day was driven by her absolute need to live on nothing. She would eat the bread little by little, day by day, letting the loaves get old and moldy, making them last. Sometimes she rubbed a little garlic on an old heel of rye bread and heated it in a pan. She never used the freezer, because with a freezer you start with something "fancy," and that was alien to the idea of "making do." Any time she made do with just a little less bread, she experienced renewed pride in not needing anything. I had missed her essential nature.

One day shortly after our restaurant encounter, she slammed the door in my face. That was the beginning of the twelve-year-cutoff. The process leading up to it is a paradigm for the cutoff, as Jeffrey Seinfeld, author of *The Bad Object*, put it: "He makes the object [other person] all bad in paranoid fashion, and then flees in schizoid fashion".

The Elements of Cutting Off:
The Bad Object

The all-bad object, what Seinfeld calls "the internal rejecting object," is like a living force within a person. That person's message, "You are bad, unwanted, dangerous, or dirty," is intolerable and must be projected outside the self. The bad object within is the force that promotes negative transference or bad feeling toward a person, place, or thing. This other person, place, or thing is bad, dangerous, or dirty. One patient referred to the thing that lived within him as a little black monster, and he saw himself as its slave.

In a rigorous choreography, the slave that houses the bad thing is allowed only a few steps. The bad thing comes forth to discover something that seems to be coming from outside which at first appears good or attractive, but as it gets closer, is discovered to be too exciting, too demanding, or too oppressive. To get closer to it means to give over to it and be overpowered by it. An alternative is to be flooded with envy or hatred of this outside thing, which is even more humiliating. The only way out is to keep away from the bad thing, and to see it as Seinfeld puts it, as "persecutory, exciting, and enmeshing."

This tyrannical dance dictates all relationships and can be maintained because the stakes are high and the means readily available: either hate oneself and feel terrible or hate another and feel good. To get away, bad feelings are projected outside the self. The real qualities of the thing that exists outside are not important, because the other soon becomes a fantasy figure costumed to appease the internal tyrant. If the fantasy figure is made to wear the dirty rags of bad and dangerous feelings, the subject can be free of them himself and can also distance himself in good conscience from the now disgusting object. These are the necessary conditions for a successful cutoff.

The Role of Projective Identification

The mechanism for placing these unwanted feelings into another person is called by psychologists projective identification. To understand its power, projective identification must be seen as a reflex, as universal and physiological, for it is as automatic and involuntary as the *startle response*, or a rush of adrenaline. Everyone projects to varying degrees. It is easier to flee from an external threat than to bear internal pain. So unless we behave as though all hateful feelings come from outside, we run the risk of being imprisoned by them.

We all try to get rid of hateful feelings. In the most intense kind of projection, projective identification, the internal reality of the subject (me) is projected into the other (you), and you must carry the feelings that are intolerable to me. In a vignette, Harvard psychoanalyst Arnold Modell tells of a woman analyst whose male patient had experienced his mother as sexually overstimulating and demeaning. Modell explains:

On one occasion when he followed behind [the analyst] into the consulting room, he told her that he wished to rape her. The intensity and immediacy of this statement were such that the analyst found it to be quite unnerving. In this fashion the analyst was forced to enter into the patient's psychic reality as she experienced a sexual stimulation that was frightening, inappropriate, and demeaning. The analyst was made to feel precisely what the patient had experienced with his mother.

The aim of projective identification is for the subject to be, Seinfeld states, "in omnipotent sadomasochistic control and never vulnerable to the object." This was accomplished in Modell's example.

Splitting and its Effects

The major mechanism within us to keep good feelings from bad ones is called splitting. Splitting is the essential mechanism for cutting off. Through projective identification, bad feelings are stored in other people and then both the bad feelings and the other person are discarded. Splitting makes experience discontinuous and obscures the sequence of actual events, so what is thrown away is easily forgotten, as it is in cutting off, for example. All shared experience with the (now) bad other must be forgotten. In his book *The Primitive Edge of Experience,* Thomas Ogden puts it this way:

> Each time a good object [person] is disappointing, it is no longer experienced as a good object—nor even as a disappointing good object—but as something bad newly discovered in what had been masquerading as a good one. Instead of the experience of ambivalence, there is the experience of unmasking the truth. "Aha. Now I see what you are." The history of the two together is now rewritten so that the present experience of the person is projected backward and forward in time, creating an eternal present just like this one (in which the truth is unmasked and the bad person given up for life). There is no other course than to banish the other for life.

Denial and Living on Empty

With the other banished, all shared experience is forgotten through denial. Ogden says, "Denial separates oneself from the dangerous object [person] by emotionally treating the object as if it had been annihilated." Distance and removal are the only way to deal with the ejected other. There is no possibility of negotiation, because there is no self left to reflect on events. It is a world of things in themselves, including the self as object. If you do not want it, get rid of it. Banished, the other ceases to exist and becomes a storehouse for one's unwanted feelings.

A correlate of denial that is often seen in cutoffs is the fervent need to empty oneself of need, such as my mother displayed. The message is, "I don't need anyone, and I don't need anything." My mother was steeped in pride from her lack of need.

Her triumph in emptiness welled up in her, and she extended her example to others and deprived them as well as herself. This is the sadomasochistic control mentioned earlier that kept her invulnerable to others. If she did without, the doorman could do without a tip or Christmas money, for deprivation enlivened her. "Who wants to be a goody-goody?" she cried with glee and emptied herself of any need for the doorman's good will. In his book *Impasse and Interpretation,* H. Rosenfeld states, "The destructive narcissist idealizes the destructive side of his personality because it makes him feel powerful," and so "any wish on the part of the self to experience the need for an object and to depend on it are devalued, attacked and destroyed with pleasure."

My mother conserved herself by sleeping late and then puttering around the house in the morning. She conserved the spectacular view of New York Harbor for herself by standing at the window for a long time, getting the good from it, and then emptying it out with her eyes before she went out. The view served multiple functions in her life, and she treated it in a more differentiated way than anything else. She ignored it, hid from it, or took it in with her eyes—or was she emptying it out?

In her bedroom, which looked out directly onto the glorious harbor, the window shade was always down. The view was central to her psychic economy, for until the end of her life she was nagged by one doubt, and that doubt, the purchase of her apartment, as mentioned earlier, was the subject of every conversation for thirty years. "The smartest thing I ever did was to buy this apartment."

In the 1960s the long walk from the subway along the cemetery to her apartment in Queens became too dangerous. When she bought a one-bedroom apartment in a new high-rise co-op, the question of whether she was submitting to someone else's control—doing what the real estate agent wanted her to do—was of course of paramount concern for her. Although she asked everyone she met whether she was doing the right thing, she confused people because another of her set pieces was to tell people, "I've made some very good investments. I'm a very rich woman, and I know what every penny is doing." People would say, "Oh, that's good. Then buy it. You can't lose."

She would lose out, she felt, if she emptied herself for someone else's benefit. If someone else made money from her weakness, she was nothing but a fool who had been emptied by a wise guy who could then boast that he was shrewder than she. Weak and a fool. Doubly a fool, a fool for wanting to live on the eighteenth floor with a view—just the kind of thing she would mock her neighbors for—and a fool for letting herself be taken in by the agent who sold her the apartment. Maybe for that reason she never seemed to be at home there. She was ashamed of having given in to its attractions. It was light and airy, yet compact. It had a functional kitchenette, a living room with a gorgeous view, and a good-sized bedroom with another gorgeous view. Yes, but what kind of fool is taken in by a view?

She took pride in wanting nothing. Because she felt it of

vital importance to be immune to temptation, she was humiliated by what she had done in buying the apartment. She punished herself by emptying herself of desires for things. Not to need anyone or want anything was what she found admirable in herself. Only having that apartment, her one mistake, spoiled that image.

My mother passed through the apartment like a ghost, indifferent to her few possessions. The older and more ramshackle these possessions were, the better, but they were not shabby enough. They did not distract her enough from the new building, the carpeted halls, the middle-class widows with their wicker plant stands, and "the person" who came once a week to clean. These were unpleasant reminders of her mistake. She boasted of the apartment to buoy herself up, but it was her one area of self-reproach and anxiety. To her, it was the one mistake in a long life, and it was one that made her look bad in her own eyes. As much as she clung to the apartment with the view, she never seemed at home, because she felt she had been a sucker.

"The view" became a persecutor for my mother, like everything in the outside world. The window shade was often down in the living room as well as the bedroom, and she never sat outside. The view menaced her day and night, like a bad introject. It gave her no peace. Yet thirty years earlier she had wanted it. Something hopeful in her about overcoming her own resistance to the bad-object world led her to take that apartment with its bustling harbor life. She may have hoped that it would bring life to her, but her own poisoned feelings about herself prevented her from having any positive experience of the outside world.

It was a circular problem: my mother lacked actual positive experience and rejected the need for such experience, and so she was locked into misery. She must have felt that her own mother could not give comfort, and that is quite possible, for my grandmother had six miscarriages or stillbirths—all boys—before my mother was born. My mother rejected her own need for what Seinfeld termed an "internal positive comforting object." My mother could not extract comfort, because she was simply unfamiliar with the feeling of comfort. She, like the tenants she mocked, would say "I've got a view" while turning away from it or keeping the shade down, or she would stay inside all day trying to consume the apartment and its view. The view had failed to yield anything good that she could hold on to, for the view, too, had become suffused with badness. Living in the apartment had become a form of persecution, a reminder from her bad introject that my mother had been weak. Even living there as shabbily as she could, she still could not atone for the shame she felt in surrendering.

Against this loss, she had one solid source of nurturance. That source was counting her money, recalculating her bank balance as dividend checks came in, and considering various new schemes to increase her bank account. She was gifted in math and seems to have used this gift in this way until her late eighties. Once, before the major cutoff, we met on the street, and she invited me to go to the safe deposit vault at the bank to meet the guard there, whom she described as "a lovely man, a peach of a guy." She signed in, he commented on her beautiful handwriting, and she gave me a happy, didn't-I-tell-you wink. She pointed out all the nice tellers she knew, including the nicest one, who was sitting in the officers' bay. Good things happen in banks, the ideal society; people move up, money moves up. Everyone she introduced me to was friendly, responding to her pleasure at being there. Two people said, "God bless you," in the smarmy way people do to the aged, and she had red spots on her cheeks from the excitement. She filled herself up on it.

She was one of those old ladies that other people liked to talk to because they found her lively manner beguiling; they were struck by her innocence and verve. A "people fix" like the one she was getting that morning would last; she need come no closer for a day, a week, or even a month. The bank officer she had hailed and the guard also benefited by having their fear of old age assuaged by such good cheer. I too felt bathed in the aura of banking goodwill and bought her pizza on the way home. Yet away from the hallowed halls of the bank, I could not hold on to her interest. Her eyes dulled, and her cheek lost its spot of color as she looked back to where we had been. Her good humor just faded.

Projective Introjection in Cutting Off

Projective identification, as noted earlier, is important for storing unwanted parts of the self in others. Projective *introjection* is a way of taking in the world again and replenishing the ego, as my mother had done when she went to the bank and said hello to the tellers. Introjection is an important mechanism for cutoffs because it does not require a relation with another person. The introjector carries around a quality, function, fantasy, or feeling within her that keeps her company, and the fantasy replaces any need for a real relationship.

My mother used introjection adroitly to take in those she was connected with while sparing herself the trouble of their company. When my children were small, my cleaning woman told me that my mother used to walk through the rooms while my family was out, opening a drawer, picking up a vase or a sugar bowl, peering at the children's clothes in the closet, looking in the refrigerator. In those days, she often took a long walk during the day; the distance from her apartment to our house was just the right length for her to manage comfortably. In the same way, looking through the things in our home was relationship enough again for her.

When my mother's sister died, my mother used her things to have an ongoing relationship with her, although my mother had not spoken to her sister in years. At the time I asked my mother if I could come and see her sometime, and she offered me this strange Faustian bargain:

"She still had the apartment?"

"Yes, I'm cleaning it out."

"Then I'll go over there with you."

"Why?"

"Nothing. Just to see. Nothing."

"Is there something special you want?"

"Just to see."

"I can't do that." (It would be an invasion of privacy.)

"I thought you wanted to come around, but you're a four-flusher like her, a faker to her dying day."

The general principle behind her activity seemed to be looking and taking in things without succumbing to envy or temptation. Nevertheless, she was testing herself fiercely, stretching herself, for she might want something. Like a window shopper, she might go inside and buy. She emerged stronger by looking into our closets and then doing without whatever it was she saw. That was her triumph. She got enough of whatever she needed of me and the children by going through our things. She continued to do this for a while after she cut off. She would not see me, but using her old keys, she came to my house. Then stopped.

Supermarkets were a natural venue for this kind of extraction in the last twenty years of my mother's life. She always bought the same things: one orange for that day, shoulder steak, and potatoes that she would cook with the steak. A small package of meat was meant to last two days. When she allowed herself something, she could enjoy it in an open, uninhibited way; she could allow herself to enjoy it. She went to several supermarkets a day when she was a little younger, but to only one during the last few months of her life. She chose the potatoes, meat, and oranges first, touching the oranges and comparing the potatoes with the ones she had bought the day before. Then she walked the aisles in what appeared to be a trance, fingering cans of soup and picking up jars to look at the price. At seventy or eighty, she compared the price of a can of soup from store to store to find the cheapest place to buy it. By this game she emptied herself of the need to have it. The whole process was an exercise that strengthened her self-sufficiency and also provided color and interest to her life. Because she was so old, she relied on whole environments—like apartments, banks, and supermarkets—to get enough to fill her need, like a whale swallowing schools of plankton. Yet even with its limitations, the system she relied on at age ninety was a creative one.

The delicatessen counter, with its meat, fish, and salads was particularly attractive to her. One day when I was with her she asked a woman who was waiting for her own order, "What do you think of these chicken cutlets?"

The woman replied, "They're very good. I got some Saturday when my son came."

I asked mother, "Should I get some for us for lunch, Mom?"

Angrily she came out of her trance: "Well . . ." and then, "No! What the hel! do you know?"

I had ruined her sport, I had ruined an interaction with another person that would have filled her for a week, I had ruined the rumination-and-rejection game. I realized that if she had been alone she would have gone on to ask the same questions about the smoked salmon, the three-bean salad, and the rice pudding, providing nourishment enough for her mind for the day. The touching, the asking, the exclamation at the prices charged nowadays, and then leaving triumphant at having bought nothing—nothing at all, not a bean, not a pickle, not a cracker—was more than enough. She was like a person on a diet who asks you, "Is that sundae good? It's butterscotch, isn't it? No? Hot fudge! Oh, hot fudge, hot fudge. I should have known! Are those walnuts? Oh, good. That's what they look like from here. I like pecans on mine, but walnuts are good too." Through this game, she extracted all the good from the situation and triumphed over it too.

The days at the supermarket together lasted for less than a month. Soon after she asked my brother to get her a home aide to shop and cook meals for her. He was also making arrangements for her to go into a nursing home, she told me (he did not speak to me or return my calls). She seemed unconcerned about the move. "We lived up, and so now we'll live down," she said, but she was not curious about the details. She and my brother were in it together, and that was enough for her.

She had no sense of "next," as Oliver Sacks calls it, and therefore she had no anxiety about the future. She "lacked the constant dialogue of past and present, of experience and meaning." She lived, as Modell explains, in a world of "the everlasting present," a world in which future time is anticipated to be no more than a repetition of the past. "Present time is expanded at the expense of past and future." Time is everlasting; there is no loss and no death. The complacency that this defense afforded her seemed to be a form of earned wisdom, although it came at a cost. "Painful memories, especially the memory of loss, are denied; it is as if the individual is effectively cut off from memories of the past and concerns about the future."

Still, she was outraged at the here-and-now, at her caretakers, who were soft-spoken Jamaican women. She locked them out and drove one away. She was becoming disoriented, and the new arrangement disoriented her further. Her psychological structure, so hard won, was toppling. By the third month of this regime, she mustered her strength only against the meddling women who cared for her.

Although my mother did not seem to mind my phone calls, she did not encourage me to visit. When I asked her what I could get for her, her cold response was, "I have everything I want, thank you." She was gathering strength. A day later she said that I had some nerve to be telephoning her when for so many years I had let her lie like a dog while I invited other people to my house for Thanksgiving. (This statement about Thanksgiving was also in her will, disinheriting me.) To this I responded, "But you called me. You left me a message to call you." She answered, "I had something else on my mind. I'm a respectable business-woman."

With the recent changes in her life, she was becoming like an archaeological dig. You did not know what level you would hit when you started talking to her. Her mental processes were often intact, and, strangely enough, her paranoia increased their func-tioning and enlivened her. For example, toward the end she was sharp, pointed, and vitriolic toward me; then she would recall some earlier event of my life to use against me. Other times she might fade, become remote, and sink into herself. She was no more and no less repetitive than she had been ten years earlier, and she told her life story in the same way that she had twenty or thirty years before.

"I did pretty good for a poor widow with no one to help me. I raised two children and worked six days a week in the busi-ness [my father had left her a restaurant supply business]. On Sundays I cleaned the house. And," she paused, "I put two children through college. How do you like them apples? Then I sold mutual funds and made a lot of money and also some smart investments, and here I am on the eighteenth floor. Pretty good for a poor widow!"

The ego is like Rome, the Eternal City, Freud said, a struc-ture that contains within it elements of earlier organizations and multiple levels of reality. "Originally the ego includes every-thing, later it separates off an external world from itself." Our present ego-feeling is only a shrunken residue of a much more inclusive connection between the ego and the world. My mother's connection to other selves was almost entirely gone. This came with age, certainly, but even before that it came with psychic iso-lation. The story of her life had only a few characters in it and only one actual incident: seeing her first banana in Hamburg, Germany, at age five. The people she remembered are surprising: her mother and father and husband. These devalued figures had disappeared from her life; she recalled the idealized figure of her grandmother without having any specific memory of her.

About her own mind she said, most poetically, "Some doors have closed." She said that there was a shadow over her mind. "I feel that they [her mental processes] are not all clicking, and I'm trying to force the issue with what I have." She was stoic about this loss. Other organic losses were compatible with her personality. For example, there was an oil painting of an outdoor cafe in Paris on the wall over her dining room table. In those last months my mother believed that the actual cafe was downstairs on the corner. Although this was an organic failing, it was consonant with the person she had been, for there had been no boundary, nor any psychological distance, between her and her environment for a long time.

Now she clung to life by renewing old injuries that were so real to her that she did not need the external world in any important way. "Who cares about you?" she said over the telephone after warning me not to come.

"I told you that I was sorry," I said.

"But I don't forgive you. You and your 'homemade soups,'" she mocked me. "Russians don't put tomatoes in [cabbage borscht]. Stop calling here." She hung up. She was impassioned. Her rage made her more alive; she was alert to injury and slight and on her guard for grievance. She was active, seeking the exciting agent. She did not succumb to depression: she fought the enemy.

Affects endow memory with significance, Freud said. More often when I phoned my mother in those last weeks she reproached me with the Thanksgiving story. I would tell her firmly that she had phoned me and asked me to call her three months before, that she had always taught us not to be Indian givers—not to give something one day and then take it back another—and that I was going to continue to phone her to find out what she needed. Besides, I said, "I always invited you [for Thanksgiving] first." She hung up, enraged, and with the aid of my own rage I said aloud, "And you never gave me a dime toward college, you mean old bitch."

Yet sometimes when I called her, she was lucid and not unfriendly. She said, "What's new?" with a lilt in her voice. She praised my grandchildren and wonderful daughters. My older daughter had gone to see her with her baby, and my mother gushed over the baby's two little teeth.

My mother surpassed me in the language of sentiment. With great satisfaction, she spoke of young girls as flowers. She said of my brother that he was "tender with me, careful with me," as though he were a lover or someone who wrapped her in silk. Yet she lived in a dusty apartment with the detritus of thirty years around her, and there was no sign of amenity—not a flower, not a new photograph, nor a box of candy from her son, no impulsive gift for the mother who celebrated him. My brother came and went from my mother's house in dust, collusive with her wish to ignore her, for she was content with her inner life.

She startled me one day when she spoke in her affected grandmother's voice, saying, "You are two little girls together," idealizing the relationship between her sister and herself, as her grandmother saw them. She also idealized President and Mrs. Roosevelt, one of her uncles, and my brother. These ideal people were a source of love and goodness for her. Growing fulsome about them allowed her to love herself. They did not threaten her or make her envious; they filled her. She loved the goodness she found in herself in recognizing these phantoms as good.

She dealt with envy by challenging herself, as she had in the delicatessen. It became a game. Contempt also served the purpose. "Come look at my roses," she sneered for years after having visited the home of a rich woman. By contempt she disavowed her envy. She sought to cure herself of envy by triumphing over material want of any kind. She succeeded in doing so by continually putting herself to the test and winning, which pumped up her narcissism. The challenge of the game inspired her, for there was something in her that started life as fun and game loving. Just as she had played solitaire every day with old shiny cards, until she died she played and won the game of wanting nothing—nothing at all.

FAMED FAMILIES
WHO CUT OFF

Reviewing her life, the writer Mary McCarthy wrote that it was a "mystery" to her why she was driven to leave husbands and lovers abruptly (she married four times). She loved her first husband but divorced him in spite of herself. In Carol Gelderman's book, *Mary McCarthy: A Life*, Mary is quoted as saying, "It is a mystery. No psychoanalyst ever offered a clue except to tell me that I felt compelled to leave the man I loved because my parents had left me. What I sensed myself was inexorability . . . independently of my will, of my likes and dislikes." She cannot quite believe it, she says, but she walks out on husbands and lovers compulsively. To her third husband, the literary critic Edmund Wilson, she wrote: "Dear Edmund, I'm sorry. This could probably all be managed with less éclat, but the only way I can ever break off anything is to run away. Mary."

Mary McCarthy's need to cut off seems to have been powered by the early death of both her parents. Yet she could never quite accept the reality of this explanation when it was offered by therapists, perhaps because she would have felt that she was making a judgment on the charming and innocent couple who had died during a disastrous flu epidemic. It happened while the family was traveling from their home in Seattle to Minneapolis. The parents became ill on the train and died shortly after their arrival in Minnesota. Mary, the oldest of the four children, was six at the time. The family was broken up, with Mary shuttled off to one set of relatives and her brothers sent elsewhere. In the upheaval her grief got lost. So many losses, so many cutoffs: from both parents, from her brothers, and from her old neighborhood, her friends, school, even the crossing guard who took her across the street every day. Everything familiar was gone. The unfinished business left in the wake of a catastrophe rarely stays buried. For Mary McCarthy and many others who have faced a catastrophic loss the sudden ending and upheaval is reenacted later. They attempt to master the loss by repeating it in other situations later in their lives.

Picasso and Age

The painful consciousness of age can lead to cutting off, sometimes in bizarre ways. Pablo Picasso cut off in this way. As he began to grow old, Picasso could no longer bear the presence of his children, so he suddenly decided to sever all ties with them. One Christmas, the artist announced to his son Claude that he would no longer be allowed to visit Picasso's home. According to A. Stassinopoulos-Huffington in her book, *Picasso: Creator and Destroyer*, his only explanation was, "I am old and you are young." Then he added, "I wish you were dead." To Picasso near the end of his life the very sight of his children was an affront, a reminder of old age and death.

Picasso's age and his children's youth brought him so much pain that he had to cut off in order to ease it. Cutting off to avoid reminders of pain can occur in other life situations, too. We think of the divorced parent who fights for custody of the child, loses the case, and illogically stops all visits to the child; of the happy couple whose child dies and who then break up because they remind each other of their son or daughter; and of the aging grandparents, with fears similar to Picasso's, who move to Florida and no longer come north to see their grandchildren, who remind them of their own lost youth and approaching deaths.

There are other examples of the pain-causes-cutoff phenomenon among both famous and ordinary families. Adoptees, children of divorce, and incest survivors often cut off from their parents and adoptive parents rather than face the complicated and painful feelings these associations invoke. In all these cases, since being around the person who they associate with pain increases their internal suffering, that person must be banished. Flight helps to maintain the barrier. It is interesting and relevant to note that cult leaders, whose followers are often cutoffs, have created elaborate religious and social structures to reinforce the barricade against the family.

People try to sidestep pain. A family may choose to blot out an event hoping to prevent the expression of pain and thus to save itself. These attempts at blotting out are not always successful.

There is, for example, the case of the family of the biologist Charles Darwin. When Darwin's mother died when he was eight, his two older sisters insisted that her name not be mentioned in the family again. John Bowlby, an expert on attachment and childhood bereavement, believed that the sisters' insistence made Darwin vulnerable throughout his life to situations that threatened family loss. Bowlby believed that Darwin responded to any illness or death in the family with illness himself. In a long and happy marriage, Darwin was cosseted by his wife, who continued to treat him as his sisters had done, at least in protecting him from loss. Even so, for thirty years Darwin suffered from chronic ill health which often prevented him from working for months at a time. The question of whether his ill health was organic or psychological has been the subject of extensive speculation. Currently, most physicians who have examined the evidence believe with Bowlby that Darwin's illnesses were psychosomatic. In Bowlby's opinion, Darwin "developed a vulnerable personality as the result of a childhood shadowed by an invalid and dying mother and an unpredictable and often intimidating father." Bowlby draws on "the now substantial body of work supporting the view that stressful life events, including bereavements, play a major role in causing emotional disturbance and disorder."

Darwin and Death

When his sisters kept Charles Darwin from seeing his mother during the two weeks before her death, they were obeying a family ethos, and it seemed to work. *Charles Darwin forgot his mother.* "I believe that my forgetfulness is partly due to my sisters," he said, "owing to their great grief, never being able to speak about her or mention her name and partly to her previous invalid state." But the Darwins were also responding to a strong family prohibition against grieving. Three generations of Darwin men, Erasmus, Robert, and Charles, threw themselves into work as a means of forgetfulness. The day after his wife died, Charles's father Robert, a physician, drove fifty miles to see a patient, leaving his older daughters to take care of Charles and his sister.

Robert never really recovered from his wife's death, even though he had experienced serious losses before. His mother had died when he was four, and a gifted older brother had died at twenty. His father Erasmus "had a strong dislike . . . [for] any display of emotion in a man," Bowlby says. Erasmus wished to control his own feelings. It was his maxim "that in order to feel cheerful, you must appear to be so."

Of his mother Charles Darwin remembered nothing except

her "deathbed, her black velvet gown, and her curiously constructed worktable."

In keeping their brother from grieving, Darwin's sisters were following the dicta of their father and grandfather, whether spoken or unspoken. The way that a family handles mourning is not necessarily discussed among family members or even consciously known to them. How close to be to one another or what to do about conflicts between members is something they automatically accept as part of the business of the family.

As we have seen, such patterns tend to exist in several generations. When the actress Margaret Sullivan committed suicide, her act was followed a year later by the suicide of her daughter.

The clearest way to see the strength of family systems is to view them with a therapeutic tool known as a genogram. A genogram is a sort of family tree which shows the history, personalities and relationships of family members. See *Figure 1, O'Neill Family Repetitive Functioning Pattern*, for a genogram of dramatist Eugene O'Neill's family.

Eugene O'Neill

The dramatist Eugene O'Neill came from a well-known family of tragic cutoffs, as the genogram shows. Alcoholism and drug abuse increased in the family over three generations, and the oldest sons died young. Eugene's oldest brother drank himself to death by the age of forty-five, and his oldest son committed suicide at the age of forty. A study by the National Institutes of Mental Health (NIMH) shows that one out of every four people who attempt suicide has a family member who has also tried to commit suicide.

Figure 1. O'Neill Family Repetitive Functioning Pattern

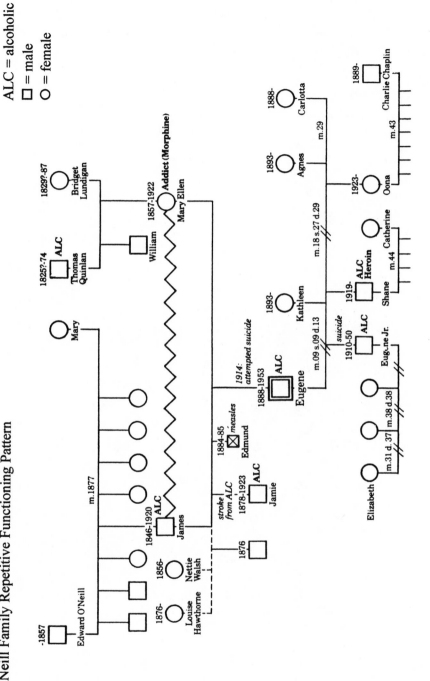

ALC = alcoholic

□ = male

○ = female

Genograms and Patterns of Success

Through a genogram one can also track multigenerational patterns of *success*. The colonial Adams family produced four generations of statesmen, including two presidents.

During the nineteenth century the Blackwell family was dominated by strong professional women who became doctors, ministers, and artists. Elizabeth Blackwell (1821-1910) was the first woman doctor in the United States. Her younger sister Emily was also a doctor. Of three other sisters, one was a writer, one an artist, and a third an invalid. Antoinette Brown, their sister-in-law, was the first woman minister in the country, and there were two suffragettes in the family, Lucy Stone and Antoinette Stone Blackwell. Of the five daughters of their brother Samuel, two became physicians, two became ministers, and the fifth was an invalid. It would be fascinating to know the attitudes in this family that produced such a pattern.

A genogram shows the dominant family theme, whether it is achievement or failure. It shows whether one member adds to the family luster or fails to shine with the others. In the family of successful Blackwell women, we notice that there was at least one invalid in each generation. Similarly, in the famous Henry James family, there were two eminent sons, William, the psychologist, and Henry, the novelist. Two other sons had marginal lives, and one daughter, Alice, was brilliant but lived as an invalid.

By rising to the challenge or falling short of it, family members tend to cluster around a family theme, whether it is achievement or agoraphobia, surgeon or suicide victim. For this reason, reading a genogram endows one with a kind of clairvoyance. Even as we look at the chart, we know that someone in the Jones family is somewhere enacting a pattern through imprinting, much as the graylag goose follows its mother's lead by listening for her call.

Humans, like any species, follow cues to survive. In the early years of life, in thousands of interactions, some cues are responded to while others are ignored. Ultimately, a pattern of response emerges. A father may speak to his child in monosyllables, just as his father spoke to him. He may expect his son to start running bases by age six because his father had the same expectation for him at the same age. He may or may not be conscious of this rerun of an old family script. In any case, certain cues are endorsed, others are discouraged, and some never appear. The cues form a pattern for a particular kind of behavior, a way of feeling, or a solution to a problem. The patterning, both physical and emotional, becomes embedded in family relationships and is continually reinforced when family members are in one another's presence. Because these relationship patterns are mostly unconscious and unnoticed for what they are, they are passed along without comment over generations. For example, in each generation and in all its branches, a particular family is hospitable to strangers, opens presents on Christmas Eve, does not talk about unpleasant feelings, does not like to travel, is a little suspicious of Catholics, expects the boys to stay in the business and the girls to leave, and so on. A pattern of customs, relationships, and expectations emerges that is embedded in all the family members and determines the way they live their lives.

Rigid Cutoffs

Rigid cutoffs are cutoffs that are irreversible. By the time the deed is done, the relationship is over. Literature is full of rigid cutoffs. Shakespeare depicts Prince Hal who, as soon as he becomes king, says to Falstaff, "I do not know thee, old man," and truly, he knew him no more.

In Anna Karenina, Levin's brother Nicolai, who had distanced himself from his brothers many times, finally writes them a note saying, "I humbly beg you to leave me alone. That is the only favor I ask of my amiable brothers." But tenderhearted Levin refuses to be cut off. As a punishment for her adultery, Karenin bars Anna from seeing their son anymore.

Pére Goriot's daughters, Anastasie and Delphine, cut off all relations with their father after they married because he was an embarrassment to their aristocratic husbands. Although they disowned him in public, Goriot's daughters still appealed to him for money. Their motives were shallow, and their attachment was shallow. Even so, they did not cut off for expedience only. They were true cutoffs, the salient fact being that they were indifferent to their father's welfare.

It is important to note that the Darwins did not cut off from one another. What they curtailed was the process of mourning. Other families regulate conflict, closeness, and mourning by expelling a member. The expulsion process was bypassed by the Darwins. What was banished was the mourning process, with devastating results within the family system.

The O'Neill family, however, showed a pattern of estrangement between fathers and children that destroyed its members over three generations. Both Eugene and his brother were estranged from their father James, and Eugene was estranged from his oldest son and later cut off his daughter Oona, after she married Charlie Chaplin. It is also common for mal-adaptive family mechanisms to intensify as the pattern passes from one generation to the next. The reason for the repetition of a pattern of cutoffs in a family system seems to be the same as the reason for the repetition of trauma in the individual psyche, namely, an attempt at mastery through repetition, and there is a compulsion to do it whether it feels good or not. When the attempt fails, the rigid family just tries harder, and, if it happens to be a family of cutoffs, it expels more people.

In the Darwin family, the beloved mother's death was so painful that she became a nonperson to them. She was someone lost to the collective family memory. As mentioned earlier, such "forgetting" is one of the ways that people try to come to terms with loss. Today, we would say that the grieving process had become stuck in denial, for a cutoff like this is the result of unresolved mourning, and Darwin's forgotten mother is not really forgotten, though neither is she integrated into the family memory. She is trapped somewhere in an uneasy limbo that invokes a kind of shame when she is mentioned. Later, there may be a return of the repressed memory somewhere in the family. Either the family body retains the memory in hiding, as in the Darwin family, or there is a reenactment in the next generation by a family member who comments on the event.

Melanie Klein and Her Daughter: A Cautionary Tale

Immigrants must become accustomed to cutting off. Losing people from one's early life is an unhappy aspect of migration. People adjust to it, suffer from it, and build it into their family system. The emigration of famed psychologist Melanie Klein from Hungary to Berlin to London was part of an old pattern in her family. Her father was born in Galicia, settled in Hungary, and later moved to Vienna. Her mother was born in Slovakia, moved to Vienna, and died in Budapest. Melanie's daughter Melitta was born in Hungary and lived in London. After the Freud-Klein controversies, she moved to New York and then moved back to London after her mother died.

The bitter hatred that Dr. Melitta Schmideberg felt and acted on toward her mother Melanie Klein had many elements. It was an idealization gone sour. It was a reaction to the death of her brother Hans (a probable suicide), which she laid at her mother's door as she had the earlier loss of her father, who had moved to another country when her parents divorced.

Melitta had other, earlier grievances. In the first years of her life her mother had left her with her grandmother for weeks at a time while she visited relatives or drifted from spa to spa searching for a cure for her depression. Later, in connection with her new career as a child analyst, Mrs. Klein psychoanalyzed both Melitta and Hans in an action that must have been felt as an insult after the mother's long absences. Melitta's deepest grievances against her mother arose from these two extremes, physical abandonment and intrusion into her psyche.

Melitta Schmideberg's Side of the Story

For Melitta Schmideberg, an essential tie between herself and her mother may have been weakened because of her mother's frequent absence from home for weeks at a time when Melitta and her brother Hans were young. Melanie Klein was an ardent mother to her daughter for the first year of her life, but as a young married woman living at the turn of the century in a cultural backwater of Hungary, with no occupation, she was bored and unhappy. She began to travel when her daughter was seven months old. For several years thereafter, Mrs. Klein was away from home for long stretches of time. While she was away, she left her children with her mother. Depressed, she went to spas for the cure or visited relatives. The grandmother openly preferred Hans over Melitta. In later years, the two older children were frequently uprooted and separated when Mrs. Klein went to study psychoanalysis in Budapest and Berlin. When Melitta was fifteen, her father had to leave Hungary for political reasons, and at this point the parents divorced. This was about the time when Mrs. Klein analyzed Melitta.

Mrs. Klein analyzed all three of her children. Melitta and Hans were analyzed as adolescents. A younger child, Eric, was closely analyzed by his mother from the time he was three. The enthusiasm of that era for freeing young children from illusions about Father Christmas, the Easter bunny, and the angels suited Mrs. Klein's own theories. Something of her philosophy as a parent comes through with Eric in a sparse account from this period of her domestic life with her children. Eric ran off several times to live with next-door neighbors who believed in the Easter bunny. The first time he ran away he was two and a half, and his mother teased him, asking him whether she should take another child to live with her in his place. When Eric said he wanted to remain with the neighbors, Mrs. Klein continued to tease him, saying that she would ask the next-door mother to keep him, which frightened the child. This anecdote shows clearly that Mrs. Klein located her own sadism in her children. (Her theory was based on the destructive instincts of infants.)

When Eric was five, his mother analyzed him every night for an hour before he fell asleep. She published the analysis as though it were a regular case history. In *Melanie Klein: Her World and Her Work* P. Grosskurth reports, "When I mentioned the identity of Erich-Fritz [Eric] to a number of English Kleinians, they expressed shock and dismay." But their reaction was part of their idealized transference to Mrs. Klein, as analyses by parents had been going on for years. Karl Abraham, Melanie Klein's analyst, had analyzed his own daughters. Freud had analyzed Anna. Incidentally, Freud had the idea that analyzing sons was more difficult. "There are special difficulties and doubts with a son," he wrote, but it is not clear why he made this distinction. That Freud, Abraham and Mrs. Klein could blithely analyze their own children is proof positive that they ignored countertransference and all of its many shadings. It also highlights their omnipotence: they could set aside their own feelings when they so wished, or so they believed.

Analyzing one's own child is neither a clinical nor an everyday transference; it is rather an invasive hybrid. (In psychoanalysis, transference is the shift of feelings experienced by a child about a parent to an analyst.) The nature of the bond between analyst and child is different from that between parent and child, the analyst being a transferential figure through whom the child works out fears and fantasies about itself and its parents. In the course of analysis, the child also learns something about its boundaries and theirs, and that it has the right to its own feelings whatever they are. In later years, a young child's analyst is either forgotten, like a transitional object (there-but-not-there), or internalized as a helper. The analyst passes through the child's life and is gone. The parent is part of the child's life forever.

No parent can objectify his or her child. There are too many layers of connection between them. Some are full of conflict, some are illusionary, and most are unknown and unconscious.

Mrs. Klein's own theory sets great store by the primitive content of all mental processes in the infant. These violent and aggressive fantasies are the basis of a relationship to the mother that is distorted. In ordinary child analysis the analyst removes distortions through play therapy. If, however, the child's play is studied by a parent/analyst who follows different rules during the rest of the day and rewards or punishes the child accordingly, play during the session of analysis becomes a performance by the child to please the parent. The distinction between what is subjective and what is objective is destroyed, and a fragile boundary has been eroded. The ordinary fallible parent is gone, replaced by the omnipotent parent, the one who can look into your mind and read all your terrible thoughts.

Mrs. Klein published a case study called "Lisa," a thinly disguised history of Melitta in which Klein attributed her daughter's lack of ability in mathematics, for example, to her castration complex. Lisa understood history to be, according to Grosskurth, "the study of relations of the parents to one another and to the child, wherein, of course the infantile phantasies of battles, slaughters, etc., also played an important part, according to the sadistic conception of coitus."

In the same vein, Klein analyzed Hans when he was fifteen and forbade him to go out with an older girl "because of the identification he was making with his mother as a prostitute." She also urged him to break off a homosexual relationship with a school friend by linking it to a sense of inferiority to his father.

Were these interdictions made by the analyst or by the mother? An analysis by the parent confirms that there is indeed no place to hide, no place where one can be whatever one wishes to be. An analysis by the parent destroys the child's subjective life.

The mother as mother has a different role. Even if the mother as analyst is not prohibiting, the mother as mother must be. Even if the mother as analyst is not demonstrably loving, the mother as mother must be. In *Playing and Reality*, D.W. Winnicott's good-enough mother is one who makes an active adaptation to her infant's needs, not the other way around. Above all, the ordinary mother lives in the continuing real present with the child. "Naturally, the infant's own mother is more likely to be good enough than some other person, since this active adaptation demands an easy and unresented preoccupation with the one infant; in fact, success in infant care depends on the fact of devotion, not on cleverness or intellectual enlightenment," says Winnicott.

In the natural order of events, the self evolves from the child's relationship with the mother. It is sometimes confusing just to distinguish what comes from oneself and what comes from one's mother. Psychoanalysis by the mother can only add to the confusion.

Melitta Schmideberg's earlier identification with her mother can be seen as defensive. Melitta went to medical school, embraced her mother's profession, and adhered to Klein's theories. It must have seemed to Melitta as though only by making herself as omnipotent as her mother would she ever be free from invasion. It was only with her brother Hans's death that the idealization of her mother's omnipotence collapsed.

These themes surfaced often during the highly public breakup of Melitta and her mother.

The Freud-Klein Controversy

Anna Freud and Melanie Klein were the two best-known child analysts in the world, and so there arose the question of which one of them would take precedence.

Two kinds of cutoff, one personal and the other societal, played themselves out in public over a period of four years. Each influenced the other and at times interlocked and created more schisms. The public tragedy of Melanie and Melitta, who finally cut off from each other altogether, affected the final outcome of the British Psychoanalytic Society.

Briefly, the theoretical conflict was over having a Freudian society dominated by Mrs. Klein and her followers, whose theories differed from Freud's. Mrs. Klein stressed the importance of the first years of life and the child's relation to its mother. Freud emphasized the importance of the father and the child's conflict with him after the age of three. The debate concerned whether Mrs. Klein had undermined Freud and his theories and replaced them with a new mythology while pretending to uphold him. The Freudians objected that Mrs. Klein used the British Psychoanalytic Society to promote her ideas, and they claimed that she was building a power base within it by cornering candidates and committees. What brought matters to a head was the flight of analysts from all over Europe to England in the 1930s and finally the arrival of Freud himself and his daughter to England.

Anna Freud stayed mostly in the background while others took up her cause. Melitta Schmideberg became one of her most vocal supporters. Neither of the Kleins was shy. Mrs. Klein was imposing and forceful in appearance and manner. Melitta was sharp-tongued. Neither was afraid of a fight. Both were indifferent to nuance. If they were heavy-handed, so be it. Neither cared about public opinion. Each believed she was right, and each was a missionary for her position. They were a mother and daughter who, at first, had shared Mrs. Klein's theories, as well as their common history. They were bound together in a thousand subliminal ways that no outsider can know, but surely part of the bitter struggle between them was an attempt to be free of what each felt the other had imposed on her.

Many years before the controversies began, Melitta wrote a farewell letter to her mother accusing her of "trying to force feelings into me." *Forced feelings* is a Kleinian expression not too different from the idea of "forced feedings." According to Klein, it means making a "forceful entry from the outside into the inside." This is not an action from mother to child, as one might think. Quite the contrary. According to Mrs. Klein, it is only the child who attacks the mother.

Melitta used the forum of the Freud-Klein controversies to put her mother on trial, forcing an actual encounter between mother and daughter, rather than an analytic one. If Mrs. Klein's account of the child's tumultuous inner life notably omits any influence on the child other than infantile fantasies, Melitta Klein Schmideberg's public reply is directed to her actual mother. She attacks Klein for her failure as a mother. Melitta denounced her repeatedly over the four-year period of the proceedings, rarely missing a meeting, and her rage never abated. According to Mrs. Klein's own theory, when a persecutory object lives inside, one never feels free, and so one must scourge again and denounce again. Melitta's quarrel with her mother and with psychoanalysis insofar as it contained her mother, never ended: the persecutor lived inside. Melitta moved to the United States after the controversies were resolved in her mother's favor, and her discontent with the analytic movement continued.

Mrs. Klein's fortitude during the protracted public debate

was remarkable, considering that every aspect of her life was under attack. Yet Klein never feared public presentation; she rose to it. As with a patient, she could be superior to the tumult. With her daughter, the resolution of their differences could only have been private, quiet, and reciprocal. Klein needed to go beyond intellectual theory to consider who they were to each other now, what the nature of their relationship had been in the past, and whether it could be mended. That she could not do. She pitied Melitta, but short of Kleinian analysis, she felt she could do nothing. Klein's own theory hobbled her. She was the authority and could not be wrong; the Society was in the child's position with her and eventually would see the error of its ways and submit. This stance may be what accounted for her celebrated calm throughout the proceedings.

After her mother died, Melitta moved her home back to England. For a time she continued her membership in the British Psychoanalytic Society. Eventually she expelled herself from the group. After her resignation, the Society settled down in an uneasy peace with its still-divided factions. Rancorous but together, the members have lived like an unhappy family under the same roof for the past fifty years. Mrs. Klein was vindicated but probably for the wrong reasons. The daughter was openly hateful to her mother, which was painful for the group, and the mother never retaliated against her daughter in public.

The controversies underlined the power of transference in the "family" and in the Society. The emotional issues between Mrs. Klein and her daughter intensified the transference struggles within the Society, prolonged the debates, and brought the issue of transference-countertransference to the fore. It is interesting that the organization's objection to Mrs. Klein was invasion, essentially the same as Melitta's. Mrs. Klein had forced her way into the inner workings of the group and had tried to take it over.

Melitta had shared her mother's views until she was about thirty, when the death of her brother triggered a reassessment of her beliefs. Six months after his death she wrote that "excessive feelings of disgust brought about . . . by deep disappointments in persons loved or by the breakdown of idealizations prove frequently an incentive toward suicide."

She wrote her mother, renouncing her own "neurotic dependence" on her mother and reminded her that "nothing causes a worse reaction in me than [your] trying to force feelings into me—it is the surest way to kill all feeling." She also sent her a check to buy out her interest in a car they jointly owned. Her letter was firm but civil, declaring her independence but also offering hope of reconnection: "I certainly can, with your help, retain a good and friendly relationship with you, if you allow me enough freedom, independence and dissimilarity, and if you try to be less sensitive about certain things." But her behavior was more militant than her letter, and their estrangement was for life.

Melitta's cutoff was unusual in that she did not flee her mother. On the contrary, she remained in the same professional circle, which enabled her to denounce her mother in the Society and to try to have her expelled. (In this way the schism in the Society then validated the cutoff of the daughter.)

Two years after the controversies ended, Melanie Klein read a remarkable paper to the British Psychoanalytic Society which appears to be an answer to her daughter's charge of "forcing your feelings into me." In this paper she coined the term *protective identification* and defines it in a way that refutes her daughter. Klein turns the concept on its head so that any given individual churns with paranoia except the observer. If the patient lifts one foot out of the quicksand, he or she is caught in it again by the other foot. The person has become entangled in his or her own projections and though Melitta may blame her mother, for example, it is her own feelings that persecute her. She can never get out.

Everyone disavows uncomfortable feelings by putting them in a container with someone else's name on them. Feelings, good and bad, are most intense between family members, and so it is hard to sort out what comes from the self and what is being induced. It is equally hard to know what parts of self one forces into someone else.

In her theory of projective identification, Mrs. Klein identified the mechanism that gives transference and counter-transference their awesome power and accounts for the strong and overriding passions that rule people's lives. Parts of the self make forceful entry into someone else and seek control. If the feeling is anger, let us say, the self is tied to the other through that feeling by angry dependence. The depth and intensity that Mrs. Klein finds in human emotions resonate with our own experience, and with hers, but she acknowledges it only in theory, not in life.

Mrs. Klein must have eventually given thought to her daughter, for as she aged, grief, loss, and loneliness were the questions that interested her. As she herself had written, "By transferring love, interest, and anxieties to new objects, the ego is able to deflect feelings of loss and mourning away from the primary object." In 1954, when Melitta's husband Walter Schmideberg died, Mrs. Klein wrote a letter of consolation to her daughter in New York. She never received a reply. Although her home was in New York, Melitta often went to Europe for psy-choanalytic congresses. Betty Joseph, a British analyst, vividly recalled "sitting on a bench outside Bedford College with Klein at the London Congress. Melitta passed them; and mother and daughter pretended not to notice each other."

When Mrs. Klein died, a photograph of Melitta as a young girl was at her bedside. In her will Klein left her daughter the family jewelry. When Klein was buried, "Melitta, unreconciled to the end, gave a lecture in London that day, wearing flamboyant red boots." Had she known about it, Mrs. Klein would have felt confirmed in her theories.

Lear and Cordelia

One of the most famous literary cutoffs of all time is King Lear, who disowns his daughter Cordelia and who is then cut off by his other daughters. One cutoff leads to many more bloody ones. Our fascination with Shakespeare's play comes from the havoc that ensues when ties with family are severed, a move that almost everyone has considered at some time, if only for a moment. It is a terrifying idea, yet an attractive one, too, because it puts an end to our feelings of obligation.

Strong feelings of love and pride lead Lear on his course. When one invests extravagantly in another, the injury or refusal is that much greater, and the wish for revenge deeper. Speaking of Cordelia, Lear severs relations with her:

> *Here I disclaim all my paternal care,*
> *Propinquity and property of blood,*
> *And as a stranger to my heart and me*
> *Hold thee from this for ever.*

And with this declaration, Lear makes Cordelia his enemy:

> *Unfriended, new-adopted to our hate,*
> *Dowered with our curse, and stranger'd with our oath.*

Being "unfriended, new-adopted to our hate" is the fate of all who have been cut off. Like Lear, those who have made strangers of them often fare no better.

5

ADOPTION:
THE SEVERED
CONNECTION

Cutting off is a basic fact of adoption, but unlike death or divorce, the loss is invisible, and so may pass without comment. The extent of loss is greater in adoption than in divorce or death, for the adopted child has lost its biological parents, its extended family, and its roots. In adoption, one family is lost, often irretrievably, and another is gained and celebrated, yet the lost family is rarely mourned. The typical adoption story, for example, focuses on the good fortune of the adoptive family, which makes it hard for the child's feelings of loss and bewilderment about the "other" family to surface. "She wanted to keep you, but when she saw she couldn't, she wanted you to have a good home," is how the story is usually told. Although true in most cases, it is the emotional dissonance of the adoptive situation that is hard to convey: that there is loss as well as gain. David Brodzinsky, and adoption expert says:

> In adoptive families, the issue of cutoff, of severed connections, is almost always of major concern, although it may well be cloaked in secrecy. The adoptive parent tends to be threatened by the shadowy figures from the child's past and the child, sensing the parent's anxiety and fear, protects the family by denying and burying his or her curiosity, concern, or longing.

Splitting

Splitting, the essential process in all cutting off, is the dominant process in adoption. Now the birthmother, now the adoptive mother—one or the other—is either good or bad, which means that all birth and adoptive relationships are tenuous. Without understanding how splitting weakens all ties in a family circle, the most well-meaning parents will continue to fail.

Splitting is the oldest and most primitive of human defenses; it separates the good from the bad. As a basic human defense, splitting, with its complicated cast of characters and its complicated feelings, seems to be tailor-made for adoption. From the beginning of life everyone has a need to put bad feelings outside (projection) the self and to take in only what is good. Splitting and projection work together from the outset; they sort experience into two large generic containers, good and bad. The good, loved mother and the bad, hated one are different people. Each has a single quality and that is that. Sorting affects the adoption process in myriad ways. The distinction of "good" and "bad" is an instinctive, dichotomous way to mark strong boundaries and keep the world safe.

If an infant is angry at its mother, its love for her is also threatened, but if the "bad" aspect of the mother has been assigned to someone else, the "good" mother is still safe, and to survive the infant must have her.

The high rate of failure in adoption has long been puzzling, but loss as the underlying cause of failure has largely gone unrecognized. There is a physical split at the time of surrender, and there are further psychic splits in the child's development after that as he or she struggles with having two families.

Having two sets of parents skews a child's development as well as the child's bond to the adoptive mother. She must shape an identity without knowing her own genealogy; come to terms with having been given away; grieve for the loss of a life in a biological family; and comfortably accommodate the idea of two sets of parents, one of which did not want her. Her adoptive mother's tie to the child is altered as well, for she feels the child's ambivalence and usually cannot find a way to counter it. The attempts of the mother and child to bond are continually undermined by psychic splits, which lead to more defensive splitting on both sides, and the connection between mother and adopted child becomes ever more fragile.

Another way to make oneself feel safe is to keep good feelings for oneself and project bad feelings onto the other person. Myths in all cultures represent the psyche in just this way: the innocent child is stolen from the humble and good mother by the evil second mother. In fairy tales the good are handsomely rewarded, and there is retribution for all wrongdoers. In these stories, our good selves and their extensions live eternally in a world that is wise and just. *Good*, *right*, and *first* (as in first-class) come into this scheme, as do their opposites—bad, wrong, and second-class—and many other unconscious pairings. In everyday life, the bad second mother metamorphosizes into stepmother, mother-in-law, adoptive mother, and witch.

Splitting is indiscriminate; everyone does it. For example, the adoptive mother, perhaps defending herself against the bad, second-mother category, splits the child into her own good child and their bad child. The psyche makes the first-level negative classification—stepmother, mother-in-law, and witch—for second mothers. Time and custom enforce the stereotypes. In her own mind, the adoptive mother does not escape the taint of being the second mother.

The Birthmother and the Child's Self-Esteem

Although birthparents are rarely mourned, often invisible, and sometimes not even spoken of in adoptive homes, the biological parents are probably alive—out there, somewhere. Thus, there is no natural closure. All adopted children carry the other set of parents within them as a part of themselves that is missing. As that loss (having a missing set of parents) is both invisible and unusual, there is no social acknowledgment of it, which adds to the feeling of injury. When the adopted child hears that someone could not keep him and gave him away, that knowledge is internalized as a primary injury to himself. Something about his self, the most precious part, has been lost. Because a small child cannot picture another set of parents, the only ones he recognizes are the ones he sees every day, and so the injury he feels is directed toward the ones he knows. It is as though the adoptive parents were the ones responsible for the injury, or abandoned him. An adopted child's investment is in his birthparents as part of himself. His birthmother, especially, holds the key to his self-esteem, and he actively struggles against identifying with his "parental substitutes."

Usually, the ordinary setbacks, deprivations, and limits of everyday life in a family are charged against the adoptive mother, while the absent natural mother is idealized. Brodzinsky reports that in one study, five times as many of the adoptees had formed positive rather than negative images of their birthmothers. The reason for this idealization is that the child's self-esteem depends upon validation by the birthmother: his best hope is that when they meet she will explain to him at last how she was forced by some outside agent to give him up. Thus, she is the only one who can answer the only question that matters: Why did you give me away?

The identification with the birthparent as part of himself changes the course of development in an adopted child. Such a child does not finally accept his adoptive parents until he has come to feel a requited love from his birthmother or come to terms with the fact that he will never get it. It is a long, stony road, and there is no shortcut: the missing part must be accounted for. As a result, the adoptive bond depends on the biological one.

Adopted Children and Attachment

Harold Brodkey, a writer and adoptee, has written, "The whole thing, the rage and rebellion of it, is nerve-wracking and scary—and close to psychic singularity—because the stakes are so odd. The tie really can be broken." Brodkey is right about the fragility of the adoptive bond. Betty Jean Lifton reports that a recent large-scale study showed that only about half of adolescent adoptees reported feeling attached to both adoptive parents, a third had been in therapy, and less than a fifth did not feel attached to either adoptive parent. Since half the parents who were asked to include their children in the study refused, the real figures may even be higher.

Security and attachment are special issues for the adopted child. If she was given away once, she might be given away again; her adoptive parents might also give her away. Or maybe her birthmother will change her mind about keeping her as her own child. If the biological parents come for her, she will have to be separated from one set of parents to go with the other. And she would have to go, would she not? Is she not related to them by blood? These questions reflect primary fears, and they do not go away just because the adoptive parents keep silent. The child picks up the cue to be silent because something terrible seems to be at stake, but her avoidance also leads to a shallow and fearful attachment.

Two aspects of development are different for the adopted child: the biological parents are the missing part of the child's self, and a deep connection is missing between the adoptive parents and the child. The child with an emotionally responsive parent knows that she is loved and develops a sense of confident expectation that the caregiver will always be available. Secure in that, the child is securely attached. Of course, this process occurs with loving adoptive parents who are eager to bond. Even so, the attachment may be brittle. What seems to be missing is the "missing" part of the child's self—his biological parents. For deep adoptive attachment to occur, the biological parents must be accounted for and integrated into her life—if only in fantasy—and remembered again and again. This, of course, is painful for adoptive parents, and so they shy away from the task. Nevertheless, there is good evidence that taking pains in this area will give them the only results they really care about: a deep connection with their child.

The "singularity" of the child's situation, as Brodkey calls it, arises from the fact that in the beginning this deep connection is missing. The adopted child is half in and half out of his adoptive family, and the adoptive mother's position is the same: half in and half out. She faces a dilemma that is unknown to biological parents: she is the child's mother and must bond well with him; she is not the child's mother until he actively chooses her in adolescence or adulthood. The child she is raising as her own—the only way to raise a secure child—is not her own. Her dilemma mirrors her child's: His adoptive mother is his only mother, yet she is only his second mother. He is identified with his adoptive family, yet his genealogy and right to life come from his birthfamily. Meanwhile, for the first twenty years of his life, let us say, his identity is formed by his adoptive parents, with whom he has only a tenuous attachment.

The Mother-and-Child Reunion

An article by Susan Sheehan, "A German Family," illustrates in detail how many of these issues play out in a real reunion. A mother and her middle-aged daughter had been separated at birth and were united through the daughter's efforts, even though the mother lived in California and the daughter in Switzerland. The mother, Else, had been told that her child was dead, and so she did not search for her. It was her daughter who placed an advertisement in a small German-language newspaper in New York City. By a series of lucky accidents, the ad brought mother and daughter together.

Finding her mother had never been far from Lily's thoughts. She often daydreamed that when she came home from school at noon that she would find a letter from her mother in the mailbox. She had searched the streets, theaters, and restaurants of Lausanne for a face that looked like her own. The task absorbed her. For Lily, life was divided into two parts: workaday duties as wife and mother and a compulsion to find her birthmother.

When it happened, their reunion was like a fairy tale, the dream of every long-separated pair: the mother found the perfect daughter, the child found the perfect mother. They told and retold their life stories; their families intertwined and prospered. Every adoptee dreams of a perfect union like this, but Else and Lily achieved it. What made it possible?

First, circumstances favored their full reentry into each other's lives. Else, a music editor in Hollywood, was close to retiring. Her husband had recently died; the child she had had in America, now in her forties, was on her own and had no children. Else was German-speaking by birth, ready to move anywhere, and so it did not matter that Lily spoke little English. Else had given birth to Lily in Lausanne when she was a schoolgirl of sixteen. Lily still lived there and had given birth to her own boys in the same hospital where she had been born, which signified a special kind of continuity. Lily's adoptive parents were dead. She was married to an easy-going merchant of Greek descent, and her two sons, now young adults, were in school out of the country. Lily's family was accustomed to making connections across national boundaries.

Both women had enough money and leisure to spend time

together discovering each other and each other's countries. Each of the families welcomed the other. Else's son-in-law built her a house close to theirs in Switzerland. In moving back to where it all began, Else, at sixty-three, made reparation by resuming the mothering of Lily, forty-seven. With all other children in their lives gone, they were exclusively mother and daughter to each other. Second, physically, Else saw that Lily was her virtual twin. Both were short and curvy; both had little feet, and both had the same nose with a small bump in the middle. As well, Else and Lily made a case for extragenetic affinity in areas that are not ordinarily thought of as genetic: they both ate and drank lightly, liked to take long walks and afternoon naps, and both liked to stay at home. Both liked cats but not dogs. Both had furnished their houses comfortably and without fuss, with working fire-places as centerpieces. Both wore sweat suits during the day but dressed simply and well when going out at night. After their first transatlantic phone call, as though some primitive ritual had been completed, both mother and daughter drank a glass of milk, even though neither normally drank milk. Else had to drive to a super-market to get it.

Together these circumstances enhanced the women's affinity for each other. It was likely, however, that their bond had already been sealed forever the first time they spoke, when Lily learned how Else had come to give her up. From the little she had been told of the events concerning her adoption and from the papers relating to it that she had found in a cabinet, Lily knew a few facts about her birthmother. These facts puzzled her: her sixteen-year-old mother had not consented to her adoption, but neither had she wanted to see her. Although this was both hurtful and confusing for Lily and it was a strike against her mother, something about the facts did not add up. She could not stop worrying about it when she daydreamed about her mother. At the same time she could not help but admire her mother's spirit, because she also knew that despite numerous beatings, Else had bravely refused to reveal Lily's father's name. Lily also felt a kinship with Else because she too had gotten pregnant as a teenager but had had an abortion. (Getting pregnant at an early age seems to have been both an identification with Else and a reproach to her critical adoptive mother who was unable to conceive.)

When Lily learned from Else that she had been placed for adoption without her knowledge, it fulfilled a primary condition for reunion without conflict: her being given up was not Else's fault. Else, like Lily, was a victim; she had been deceived. She had believed that her child had not survived, and her family had continued the cover-up to the present time, even though Else was now sixty-three years old. All her life she had blamed herself for the death because in her shame she had hidden her pregnancy by tightly corsetting herself and had lain on an icy mountainside overnight in an attempt to kill herself. She knew she must have killed the baby. Lily learned that she had not been given away because she was unlovable, which is every adoptee's fear.

Since neither Else nor Lily was responsible for the separation, they were both able to transcend the greatest psychological barriers to reunion—shame, guilt, and the self-hate of surrender. In this case, Lily's self-esteem was fully validated; her mother really wanted her but had been tricked into giving her up. Else's own self-hate, believing that she had killed her baby, was redeemed by Lily's search, blooming health, and good life. Full of joy and free of guilt, Else and Lily sought out Else's mother.

Everything has its season. Else's mother, Mrs. Siegel, now in her nineties and mentally intact, was pleased but unsurprised to meet Lily after forty-seven years. She was still convinced that she had done the right thing. Jews were being persecuted in Germany at the time of Lily's birth, and they had all had to leave. Still, Else and Lily pressed her: why did Else have to give up her baby? Why? A girl of sixteen with a baby might not get a visa for America, Else's mother explained, and even if she did, she certainly would not have been able to find work there. Yes, but after so many years, they countered, why had she never said a word about something so important to Else? At ninety-one, it was clear that Mrs. Siegel had planned to go to her grave in silence. Placidly, she said, "That was the way we did things then"

The Adoption

Lily had been adopted by a well-off Swiss-German couple, Claire and Werner Schmutz. She was their only child. Werner Schmutz had wanted a child and chose her from a hospital nursery. As Lily remembers it, her mother, Claire, had no maternal feelings and had no patience for a naughty child. Their skirmishes were about demeanor, being respectful, and dressing well. Lily says that Claire wanted a miniature well-behaved grown-up, a docile companion. When Lily was four, the Schmutzes took a boy from the same hospital nursery on a trial basis but sent him back because he was "dirty." Lily felt that her adoptive father was affectionate but submissive and would not stand up for her. Apart from a lavish engagement party that the Schmutzes gave for her and their pleasure in the man she married, Lily seems to have few warm memories of her adoptive parents, and her connection to them ended with their deaths.

One question remains about Else and Lily's idyllic reunion: what happened to Lily's feelings for the man and woman who had been her parents of forty-seven years? She knew that "Claire [her adoptive mother] trembled all her life that I would seek my mother and find her, or that my mother would turn up to claim me." Claire must have been attached to Lily, although Lily did not feel attached to her. She did not love her adoptive parents but felt indebted to them, and so she had waited courteously until they died before she began her search for her birthmother. Otherwise, Lily never had any conflict at all about looking for her.

When Lily was eight, she learned from a classmate that she had been adopted, and from that day Lily says that she lived in "two compartments." Lily's lost mother became a part of her ideal self, which was one compartment; the workaday world of the Schmutzes and her life with them was in the other. The adoption was good news to her because it explained her shallow attachment to Claire and allowed Lily to lose herself entirely in her fantasy mother. It was bad news to Lily because Claire had never told her she was adopted, which added to the distance between them. Claire had, however, told Lily the little she knew: that her mother was a schoolgirl, that she would not reveal the name of Lily's father, and that she had not consented to the adoption.

As Lily saw it, she and Claire were a mismatched pair: Claire was brittle, nervous, and fastidious; Lily was a normal, high-spirited child. Claire was an uneasy mother, whether biological or adoptive. She thought that children were unruly and difficult; she had refused to adopt a second child when the little boy turned out to be dirty; and she would sometimes wait for Werner to come home to change Lily's diaper if the maid was out. She complied with her husband's wish to adopt Lily, but perhaps she could not face her own ambivalence—was it not natural for every woman to want a child? She could not transform Lily in her own mind from unwanted to wanted child. As it was, they quarreled bitterly; Lily either fought her mother or fended her off. Her picture of Claire is poorly supported by memories and seems one-dimensional. Perhaps because they were often at war, Lily could not remember earlier, more loving days with Claire. When she was eight, Lily withdrew even further from Claire because Claire had not told her that she was adopted.

Yet Claire would have had her own fears. In the 1940s, there were no adoption networks, as there are today, and few books on the subject. Adoption was catch-as-catch-can and often clandestine. Couples had no idea that adoption was a lifelong process that began, not ended, with the legal decree. As often used to happen, the adoption was casual, and the family was on its own too soon after taking the baby home. To them, in contrast to today's more informed public, adoption was a single act, like divorce, best done quietly and quickly. There would have been few adoptive couples in Lausanne to serve as models, and adoption itself was vaguely shameful because it called attention to a couple's infertility. One should install the baby comfortably, it was felt, have a viewing, and behave like everyone else who had had a child in the normal way.

The Adoptive Mother

The story of Claire and Lily is the story of an adoption that did not take. Brodkey says fatalistically of his own adoption, "An adopted child does not carry the shadow of his adopted parents inside himself." In other words, adoptions never take, and nothing can be done to prevent drift, attenuation, and cutoff. Yet the Schmutzes do not prove the point: they began with drift: Werner wanted a child; Claire was not sure and tried to control her own anxiety by controlling the baby. By the time she was eight, Lily's parents had not told her that she was adopted. In contrast, a biological mother has a long pregnancy, an intimate relationship with the fetus, and the support of a whole community of women in making the transition to motherhood. An adoptive mother has few reminders and few models of what is to come, and so she must prepare for the child by conscious awareness. She must transform herself into a mother who is waiting for the child who is coming. As in a biological birth, that child is the right child.

A true mother, biological or adoptive, feels her way into the infant's experience of being wet, cold, hungry, or afraid, but she is sometimes prevented from bonding by life circumstances. For example, an adoptive parent may fear attachment during the legal waiting period. (In the case of the Schmutzes it took four years.)

Even without these difficulties the adoption story adds another parameter to bonding: a child is secure when he feels well protected by idealized parents, and current research has established that that feeling is not firmly in place until the age of seven, when the child can understand what adoption means. What the child hears in the adoption story, however carefully it is said to him, is that he was sent away once and is in danger of being sent away again. Losing a parent early in life feels like abandonment and mobilizes intense fear and rage.

Claire "trembled" that Else might return when Lily was a child, just as much as Lily wished for it. Yet Else's return would not have guaranteed a happy ending for Lily, either, because feelings of abandonment cross all lines. We know, for example, that in cases of babies switched at birth, young adolescent adoptees have intense conflict about returning home. It is the process of cutting off from either set of parents that seems to override the need for a just outcome. Indeed, in such cases, it is hard to know what outcome is just or what outcome would even feel right.

When there really are two mothers, a birth and an adoptive mother, it is easier to split them definitively into good and bad rather than deal with nuances. One is a good mother and one is a witch. One is a natural mother, and the other is a stepmother. One is a "real" mother, and the other an adoptive mother. Because our emotions are highly colored and not subtly tinted, we have to keep reminding ourselves that reality is both good and bad. In real life, it is the same good mother who sometimes behaves like a witch, for even the most devoted mother is exhausted by the never-ending job of mothering. The flesh-and-blood mother who is on the scene is both good at mothering and bad at it, sometimes attuned to what the child needs and sometimes not. She is responsive and self-absorbed, devoted and neglectful. The picture is mixed. What matters most is that she is available to the child over the long haul. What matters is the core of connection, which is everyday fidelity.

For example, in everyday life, Claire, the adoptive mother, is also the real mother, the one who says no and the one who has hidden the news of the adoption. The ordinary setbacks and limits of everyday life in a family are charged against the mother who is right there; the absent natural mother is idealized. In addition, Claire acted out her fears and uncertainties by quarreling with Lily over small matters and refused to deal with the big one, so the relation between them was troubled well before Lily found out about her adoption. From the time she heard about her biological mother, Lily's daydreams were centered on that mother, and she withdrew from her adoptive family and lived in a secret world: her other mother would not have lied to her about the adoption; her other mother would not be so strict. As Christopher Bollas, the British psychoanalyst, has pointed out, when an important aspect of the child's self is ignored, her development in that area is arrested. Bollas concludes:

> When a parent refuses to perceive, identify, address in speech and facilitate through attitude or action an element presented by the child to the parent, then this aspect of the child's self may be left in isolation: apparently unnoticed, uncommented upon and with no facilitative resolution. If so, the child is stuck with a self state that registers not simply an arrest in his personal development, but an arrest in the parent's parenting as well. No child, in my view, develops a point of fixation by himself: one must speak of a family point of arrest and fixation. The parents' refusal to address a part of a child to some extent amounts to an implicit "let it be" or "he is just that way" which later on becomes the nature of mood experience: let's just let him be while he is like this.

Lily's adoptive self was left in isolation, uncommented upon and unresolved, just as the Schmutzes had been left in isolation when they got Lily from the hospital. No doubt, too, that the Schmutzes wanted to spare Lily the pain of knowing, yet grieving over the loss of her biological parents would seem to be a necessary step in order to avoid living life in two compartments, as Lily had come to do. From the time she was eight, Lily lived in a secret and adamant state of withdrawal from her parents. If she had ever carried the shadow of her adopted parents within herself, it disappeared once she learned of her adoption.

Brodkey, who as an adoptee, speaks of these shadows, was taken to live with his adoptive family when he was eighteen months old. He sensed even before he was two that he was on trial and tried to make himself agreeable. ("The Child Has Not Been Adopted Yet" is Brodkey's ironic subtitle to one story.) He wrote what it felt like to see and touch these large, strange, exotic, and frightening creatures, these new adoptive parents; his fictional name for himself was Wiley, for he had spent his entire childhood in pretense, outwitting them. Secretly, he was still joined to his mother, for the loss of his ideal state was part of his life with her. "What I am is her twisted and altered and bereaved and ignorant heir. She died when I was two. I died as well, but I came to life again in another family, and no one was like her, everything was different." Unaware that a child can feel grief, the new parents unwittingly sponsored his shutdown. Although Brodkey officially learned about his adoption when he was six, and Lily when she was eight, neither felt in harmony with the adoptive families they grew up with. There are two possible reasons for this, which would have a similar effect in similar cases: (1) the children were falsely, overtly, identified as adopted children only, and their biological identity was denied them; (2) they had to work through their biological identity before they could fully accept their adoptive parents, and if they were kept from doing so, it acted as a developmental arrest; they would never accept their adoptive parents.

We know from the psychoanalyses of some adopted children that the process of integrating two sets of parents occurs little by little, and grief over loss is an inevitable part of the process. The child first sees himself, according to child analyst, Paulina Kernberg, as "the natural child of false natural parents, that is, of the adoptive parents." Second, the child perceives that he is the natural child of absent, idealized natural parents. The adopted child thus actually lives the family romance that other children live in fantasy: that is, he is from a noble family somewhere out there and has been placed with this disappointing family, which will never understand him. In time, the biological child grudgingly realizes that the loving mother and the depriving mother are one and the same person. The adopted child, however, never has to face that reality unless it is called to his attention. Thus the good mother-bad mother split continues.

The child's dearest hope is that someday he will miraculously find his real family, at which point his life will change. (This was "the family point of arrest and fixation," Bollas mentions, which later, with rare good fortune for Lily, metamorphosed into an idyllic family romance.) If she had known about her adoption and been able to work it through little by little, Lily would have realized that she feared or devalued her adoptive parents. Finally and ideally, the child achieves an emotional acceptance of both sets of parents and integrates the two sets of relationships. Therapy points to the task: integration, but it may take more than therapy to do it, for often patients with early childhood losses still have a compelling need to seek out and reclaim the lost person, or at least a symbol of him in the real world.

Early loss is like the loss of a body part, only it is a loss of a part of the self: the part of the self that soothes and comforts. The search is an attempt to restore the loss and it may be that the adoptee who must search does so out of a memory of her mother's body. The real-life search in the world captures something more concrete and more directly related to the person who was lost for the searcher than therapy can.

When someone close or familiar is no longer there, babies who have been in foster care or who have been cared for by their biological parents for even a few months will notice that their environment has changed, even though they may not be aware that a specific person is no longer there. Even a baby of six to nine months will begin to have a perception of loss. In an article from *The New York Times Magazine* titled "I met my daughter at the Wuhan Foundling Hospital," Bruce Porter tells Zoe's story. When she was nine months old, Zoe was abandoned in a shipyard on the Yangtze River in China. Two months later she was adopted by Diane Reichman, a schoolteacher from New York City. When she was a toddler, her mother took her to a restaurant in Chinatown. The waitress spoke to her in Mandarin, and Zoe seemed to understand. Shortly afterward, she cried hard over nothing. "She went on for half an hour and there wasn't anything I could do to make her stop," Reichman says. "I'm convinced that that experience triggered some deep memory, and that the crying was a delayed expression of the sadness she felt over what she had lost."

Zoe's tears almost seem prophetic, for an adopted child has formidable losses from the start. Her mother has an equally formidable task: she is the only one who can help Zoe with her losses, which means acknowledging that Zoe has two families. At the same time, this psychic split must not weaken Zoe's strong attachment to her adoptive parent, because her own strength depends on it. Some adoptive parents have also learned, especially in recent years, that psychic splits easily translate into cultural ones, and into class war.

The Second Mother

The adoptive parent can also be seen as a villain for reasons of social class. The fact that she can usually provide for the child materially, is not necessarily in her favor. It is as though it gives her an unfair advantage (which is bad) over the birthmother (who is good). Money is seen as grubby, just as the baby is ill-gotten, because money has changed hands for the child. When no money has changed hands, the legal papers or the fact that the adoptive parents have raised the plane fare to go to a foreign country for the child become suspect. According to such a view, the whole transaction is rotten, and only a fairy tale ending can make it feel right: namely, that the adoptive parents see the error of their ways as soon as they are handed the baby, return her to the trembling young mother along with an enormous check to provide for the child's college education, and discreetly tiptoe out of the room, never to look back. This scenario redeems everyone, including the adoptive parents, who have been cured of their rapacious ways. This script, far-fetched though it seems, is attractive to many adoptees and birthmothers who feel that adoption is the worst of all solutions. Heal the split by abolishing adoption, they say, for its wounds are incurable, and almost any arrangement that keeps the child with its mother would be better. Are they right?

There are about five million adoptees in the United States, or 2 percent of the population, but they constitute 5 percent of the outpatients in mental hospitals and 15 to 20 percent of inpatients. Each of these adoptees has in common the loss of a biological parent. The cutoff influences the course of their adoption in several ways:

1. The child feels a primary injury at having been given up for adoption; the adoptive parents are only "second parents"; and the child invests part of himself in his birthfamily.

2. There is increased alienation on both sides: the child is alienated because he cannot use the adoptive parents as idealized protectors, and the parents are alienated because their parenting functions have been undermined.

3. Because he cannot use their protection, the child comes to feel that he has been abandoned by his adoptive parents too and so "divorces" them. Without a strong idealized attachment to his adoptive parents, his core identity is fragile.

4. Abandoned by one set of parents for whom he yearns, he also "divorces" the second pair of parents at an early age. This split increases his feeling of alienation.

5. The adoptive parents feel like failures, which alienates them further. In truth, however, it is the whole system, unexpressed, that dooms them all to failure, victims of the double bind: they are the parents and must nurture the child as their own; they are not the parents and must never forget that the child is on loan.

The cutoff from biological parents, the complicated development issues for adoptees, and the double-bound and alienated adoptive parents all help to explain the high rate of failure of adoptions better than either nature or nurture, alone or together. This does not mean that adoption is doomed to failure, only that the splits, cutoffs, and double binds, heretofore hidden from view in adoption and prevented connection must be exposed to the light. A deep connection to the adoption process is the best defense, for in adoption, consciousness is all, and a healthy outcome depends on an awareness of its pitfalls.

6

CUTTING OFF
DURING DIVORCE

Divorce creates distance in megaleaps: old relationships, even those that seemed rock solid, cannot withstand the uprooting of home, school, jobs, neighbor, and everything familiar to the family: father, mother, and children. The parent who becomes the noncustodial parent most frequently is the father, so I will use him as an example. He is outside the ebb and flow of daily experience and becomes less real to his children. He is either devalued or idealized. They are less real to him, too. "It's like television," one father said. "I see them in sound bites." When he does see them, they bring a nagging reality to their meetings that makes him feel helpless and used. They need gym shoes or a winter jacket, money for the school fair, or a hockey stick. They have resentments about friends or enemies on the block that they do not want to talk about, but they smolder over them secretly during his precious time with them.

Distance adds a different hurt, a feeling of abandonment and yearning that is a little unreal because, although father is gone, he is still in their lives. The family environment has gone with him, and there is a frantic search for somewhere to go, some way to be together that has the feel of family, and some way to replace what has been lost. Going to the circus is not family. Family is watching your children grow day to day. Seeing them only on weekends, the father is under pressure to organize the time with his children so that it is well used and to remember what they like and do not like. Seeing them less often, however, he does not know the little daily things about them, which they silently record and hold against him. Suddenly, they are sullen; they come to meet him looking like refugees and have nothing to say. He has to do all the work. If he complains about their behavior, their mother gets snippy. Anyway, frankly, seeing the children reminds him of their mother and, though it is not their fault, he is tempted to put that big mistake, his marriage, behind him, once and for all. Whether he jumped or was shoved, he is lucky to be out of it: there is no respect here, and everyone is out for themselves. He is nothing to them except what he can buy.

Later, the divorced father sees the support of his children—for example, paying for college—as a voluntary act, and, in most cases, not a compelling one, given that he has already paid thousands of dollars in child support. This is very different from the situation of the middle-class undivorced father, who lives with his children and does not question his obligation to them. The distancing that comes with divorce changes a father's view of his "obligations."

Distancing grows out of the man's dealings with his ex-wife. Each time they confront each other, it is hard for him to remember anything good about her. He used to have mixed feelings about her, especially when they were trying to separate and came back together for the sake of the children. Now, in the continuing battle over money and housing, he sees that she was manipulating him from the start. He asks himself what he ever saw in her. The more he thinks about it, the worse it seems. He is sure of only one thing: his ex-wife was good at putting on an act. He then projects the present experience with her backward and forward to create a past that is as bleak as today. In this mode, there is no other course than to banish her from consideration.

Why Fathers Divorce Their Children as Well as Their Wives

One of the most puzzling aspects of divorce is that fathers who were close to their children before a divorce disappear from their lives five years afterward. One year after the divorce more than half of all divorced men stop paying child support. Emily Visher and John Visher, experts on divorce and remarriage, have noted that society silently accepts (or perhaps is merely resigned to) this state of affairs, and so this is one of the most common forms of cutoff, although not always defined as such. Five years after divorce, research projects no longer bother to include either the nonresidential parent who lives at a distance or the one who either never sees the child or sees her only rarely.

After divorce a father finds himself in the unfamiliar roles of visitor and entertainer. Before the divorce he is at the center of daily life, the head of the house, but after the divorce he is only a drop-in provider. Before there was structure; after there is none. He has to invent a way to have a relationship with his own children. This is humiliating. He wants to be a father and tries to be a good one, but, without ordinary daily contact, the connection between him and his children grows weaker. No matter what the actual circumstances of the divorce, the children feel that he has deserted them.

In the first several months after separation his visits are stilted, awkward, and angry, and every outing an unhappy reminder of better times. The father is at a loss to explain to them why their mother has custody—which is the case 90 percent of the time—at least not in any way that he can believe himself. Noncustody is like a judgment on him that he has failed to do what a man should do, which is to stay with his children. He believes in keeping contracts and not quitting when things get rough, so how could this happen? At one time it was unthinkable to him; he was close to his wife and her family. They were always kind to him, and she was his best friend. Now they do not speak to him anymore, and one of the kids let it slip that they speak badly of him. There is no way to fight it, what with the judges and the money, and the moving and the upset, and the kids' sour looks. Sometimes the divorced father feels the urge to get out and start over, and more and more frequently he does.

According to Judith Wallerstein and Sandra Blakeslee, in a study of the family situation ten years after divorce, 65 percent of the children had poor relations with the fathers, and many had lost contact with them altogether. This percentage is too high to go unnoticed. What is the reason for it? Can anything be done about it?

Dissociation

One of the cruelest results of divorce is that former lovers become nonpersons to each other in an unconscious move to spare themselves pain. It is too painful to feel concern for some-one you cannot control. Through distancing, dissociation, and a mental change of category, lovers become strangers, then objects (like turnstiles—a way to see the children), and then nonexistent, or as someone they "used to know." When there is continuing conflict and the ex-spouse is the hated enemy, she is quickly depersonalized and becomes a *dangerous* object, not just a dis-carded one. As a loving wife, she was part of his good feeling about himself; as an enemy, she can be annihilated. (This is true for the wife as well. To battle her husband, she annihilates the person she used to love, but the children she has from the marriage redeem the past.) Without realizing it, he identifies the children with her, with her clamor for money and goods and schools. Wife and children together are always pushing his buttons. Any exchange with any of them can put him in a bad mood for hours, and he finds that he does not answer his phone anymore and goes away on those weekends when he does not see his children.

When a couple is first married they both feel closer to each other than they do to anyone else. "They" are a unit, everyone else is an outsider, an "other." Thus, family life continually reinforces the already powerful innate pattern of taking in what is good and expelling what is bad. As a marriage unravels, this process reverses. What was close becomes distant, then foreign, and then nothing (or something dangerous). In the process of dissociation, connections, continuity, and consistency are lost, and a sense of identity changes. The man who was married to Linda, with all that that entails, becomes Tom, who is single again. Linda becomes "someone I used to know," and Linda's identification with Tom also becomes part of a dim past. Dissociation sneaks up on them and takes them unaware. A 1992 issue of the *Harvard Mental Health Letter* states, "Old memories, feelings, and perceptions are stored in separate compartments or are buried in oblivion from which they may suddenly emerge." Before they know it, someone important is no longer part of the self.

How Dan, a Divorced Father, Dissociated

Even before he moved out of the house, Dan had left his marriage in his mind when he focused his attention elsewhere. It was not that hard to do, because when he sat down at his desk and turned on the lamp, everything else disappeared. Sometimes he felt as though he were hypnotized by work, very low-key, and receptive to ideas, which is a nice kind of amnesia. Anyone or anything outside that immediate context came as an unwanted interruption.

Work saved him. The rhythm and focus of tasks (like filing tax returns for his two stores on time, without giving away anything to the government) supplanted a gray, formless depression that Dan experienced (namely, the combined effect of his time in Vietnam and his broken marriage). Depression hung heavy on him whenever he had time on his hands. He felt good when he finished his task and signed his name and put a check in an envelope just before midnight of the last filing date.

Now that the divorce is final, Dan plans to enlarge his business, and so he often works late. (His ex-wife, Ellie, has gone; she has moved out of their house in the suburbs—not without a fight—to an apartment in the city.) She is tight-lipped and accusing about her apartment—"this hole," as she calls it. The children go to a parochial school, and the school fees are a new noose around Dan's neck. He concentrates so hard on specifications for two new sites he is planning that he works until late on Friday night, forgetting that he had promised to take his son, Drew, bowling. While he is working, he thinks vaguely that there is something he has forgotten, and an image of a buzz bomb crosses his mind, an image that has been there before and that he manages to blot out. Again he thinks with pleasure of how he managed to find a legal loophole in his taxes and figures out again that he has probably saved about $4,200. He does not remember Drew until the phone rings.

Losing People in Your Mind

Several kinds of forgetting are mixed together in this episode; most are unconscious. Dan dissociates so that he can get a job done, and he succeeds, which is gratifying and reinforcing. When a war memory begins to surface unbidden, he is able to leave it and concentrate on a difficult and mildly painful task, which is doing office work late at night. This pain is better than a war-memory pain, and he can tolerate it and even court it because he can master it and has something to show for it.

Sometimes he is even conscious of it and will say, "After Vietnam, even banging your head against a wall feels good."

Being able to master small pains makes him feel in control. Dan often works nights now that he is divorced, and he is aware that it is better to be in his own shop than with his sullen and angry son or his ex-wife. It is even better to be working than to be in his own new place, which is bare and dusty. In his mind, he sees his son in the apartment slamming a ball around in the empty space of the rooms. He simply does not know what he is going to do with Drew when he picks him up for the weekend. At this thought he blanks Drew out as he would a war memory. As he begins to think of the appointment with his son, he is afflicted with a pain he cannot master, and he forgets him again and plays a computer game.

Slowly, wife and son move into the "Vietnam" category. Drew merges with Ellie because the two are both accusing and aggressive and make him feel helpless. Frankly, when he sees one, he thinks about the other. He knows he cannot stand Ellie because of all she put him through, but it seems to him that the boy, who was always a chip off of the old block, is now becoming more like her. He even whines like her.

As time goes on, Dan works harder to meet his child payments, and his business thrives. Ellie finds out that he is opening a branch in a nearby city and wants more money. Their lawyers meet. Then there is a hassle over whether Dan will pay for Ellie's lawyer so that she can sue him for more money. The judge almost agrees, until Dan's lawyer screams bloody blue murder. That's family court, for you, he thinks; always on the woman's side. To look good with the feminists they will squeeze you dry. Then Annie, their little one, says, "How come you're not crying all the time? Mommy's always crying." This is a downer. They are not supposed to mention each other to the kids, and he, at least, keeps his mouth shut.

Dan has to decide where to put his time now that the two

new stores are opening, the one downtown a mile-and-a-half away and the other twelve miles away in a neighboring city. Dan says that since he is not a family man anymore, Joe, his partner, can stay close to home, and Dan will stock the stores and hire staff. He does not mind; he likes the drive and the distance. It takes him away from his troubles.

When Ellie ruins things for him once too often, accidentally on purpose—like the time she told him that Annie's birthday party was on a Sunday instead of a Saturday, and he showed up on Sunday and found his child heartbroken—he decides to fix Ellie's little red wagon and set visitation days himself, not giving her much warning. That way she cannot play games with his head. He is just not going to lie down and play dead anymore, and that is for damn sure. He also will not tell Ellie where he is taking the kids or how long they will be gone, playing dumb when she asks, "Then how do I know how to dress them or when to be home?" He likes himself better for standing up to her like a man.

When he begins spending three or four days a week at one of the stores getting it organized, he gets calls from Ellie about how he is not seeing the children enough. Dan asks her whether she wants him to take them out to the movies or to have the extra money instead? Then she "reviews" the situation: "When we first separated, you saw the kids three times a week, then twice a week until you started to 'forget' about Wednesdays, and then after we went to court about support payments, you took it out on them and saw them only one day over the weekend."

Dan does a little reviewing too and answers, "Who busted my chops every time I tried to take the kids or wanted to spend a weekend with them at my sister's house when the whole family was coming?" Then Ellie has to tell him that his sister went out of her way to say that Dan was looking ten years younger and was working out, that he had got a new blue blazer, and what else? He interrupts her here, thinking about the woman who runs the boutique down the street from his new shop; she's none of

Ellie's business, and it's strictly platonic so far anyway. Ellie is the one who wanted the divorce, so let her shut her mouth. Aloud he says, "But if we're talking about who did what to who, what about when I got my apartment with nothing in it and you still had the house? I asked you as nice as pie if I could spend my time with the kids there with their things. How many times can I take them to see *The Lion King* anyway? And you said to me, `Divorce is no picnic.' I'll never forget that, Ellie."

Dan was thinking it was about time he expressed his anger; she had some nerve, anyway, telling him when and where to see his own kids and snooping around to find out if he had a girlfriend. Now his contempt for her begins to insulate him from the hurt she used to cause him when he cared about her. In fact, each time he thinks about her now he despises her more. He thinks, how can you mind losing someone you despise? You cannot, and you do not. When you hear her name, there is just a dark mass of feeling. No person, no nothing.

When Dan still loved Ellie he was vulnerable because it hurt (as he found out) when she abandoned him. She had him at her mercy and under her control. Some of the predivorce fights—the name-calling, the hang-ups, the scenes—were her way of testing whether she was still in charge of him. He feels he would rather die than put up with being led around by the nose anymore.

Dan's difficult adjustment to his new status as a divorced father is not unique. It differs from many other divorced men and women only in the details. He feels that he has been ejected from family life, devalued, and used by the people he used to love. His pride in himself as a man who takes care of his family has been shattered. These are some of the major reasons why men who are divorced and don't have joint or sole custody move further and further away from their children.

Pride

Robert May, a psychologist who has examined male fantasies in depth, finds that pride is the engine that moves many men. At their cores, many men are acutely sensitive to being shamed and have a driving urge to look good in the eyes of other men. This fierce pride is rooted in an attempt to become like their fathers, separate from women, and out from under the control of women. Being powerful defines their feeling of worth. A man's pride in himself is rewarded when he does something on his own or with men like him; applies himself to a difficult task; and fixes, changes, or improves something.

In the family, the majority of such men continue this executive and technical work, connecting it to the outside world. They are usually curious about things, not people, and part of their pride in themselves is to figure out by themselves how things work, like a car or a dishwasher. Men should know things without being told and cannot say, "I don't know." Women do the inner work of the family and bring the world into the home through the telephone and their network of other women. Although these days most women work outside the home, the different roles of men and women have not changed substantially.

When, as Wallerstein and Blakeslee call it, "the mother-wife-link keeper," is gone, it is not easy for most men to take on the tasks of women, because the new skills that men must learn after divorce when caring for children are largely unfamiliar and awkward to them. They have to find the answers to social and people-linked questions. Before divorce, the marriage itself provided the feminine and social side that enabled such a man to be a loving father, and he, secure in the marriage, grew with the structure. After divorce, the old intermediary is gone, and the man has to deal directly with the children himself or through a network of child-care providers and sitters. A divorced woman may have trouble doing the tax returns for the first time and may well find the task onerous, but she will rarely be embarrassed by it. Because most women do not mind asking for help, doing so only adds to their skills. Men, on the other hand, are historically supposed to know everything without asking. Autonomy is, by such a definition, a matter of a man's pride, and part of a man's burden is to do things well and gracefully the first time to prove that he is self-sufficient. He usually feels as though he is being observed by another, more competent man, which adds to his burden. If he fails in performing a task, he cannot forgive himself: his failure is a sign that he has not lived up to his own ideal, and he imagines that he looks small in the eyes of other men. As a result, a broken marriage that cannot be fixed, or clumsy visiting arrangements with the children, are reasons for terrible self-reproach. Such failures recall memories of the man's past humiliations and raise the specter of a more crippling vulnerability to come. In their hearts, having traditional values, men then expect things to end badly. Robert May discovered that when the men he studied made up stories their fantasies began in physical and emotional excitement and even pride but soon collapsed in failure and despair. The stories started with élan but ended with sorrow, while stories told by women went just the other way; they started badly but ended well.

Biology and Men's Lives

Men are more aware of life's limits. From the moment of conception, they are more vulnerable to death and disease than women. Stillbirth, miscarriage, infant and childhood diseases, learning and maturation difficulties, alcoholism, suicide, and the incidence of sudden death all occur at higher rates for men than they do for women. Even monks who lead cloistered lives die early. Men are less orgasmic than women in their fifties and sixties (a sign of decline for most men); in general they die earlier, and die even earlier if they live alone. Single women who live alone live longer than married women. Some of the qualities that May notes, like a reverence for success and power, appear to come from knowing that life is short and a feeling that they must move fast to make their mark. Women are often exasperated by men's particular sensibilities, but one way to think about men's pride is to realize that in every sense men have no time to lose. After divorce, most men move on quickly—half remarry within the first year—and many of those ensure their posterity by having more children by women younger than themselves, even if they themselves are not going to be around to see these children mature.

The Social Psychology of Men and Men's Fantasies

The differences between men and women, according to current research, affect the way they behave after divorce. The strongest bond in life is between mother and child, and, for a boy, this earliest "divorce" from his mother is the hardest to accept. For a girl, the loving bond she feels with her mother feels right and comfortable because she discovers early that she has been nourished by someone like herself and one day will do the same for her own child. This discovery is dissonant for the boy, who according to May, "discovers that he owes his life to . . . an Other." He must pull himself free of her and all things feminine because he is not like her. After the initial disappointment that he cannot have babies like her, he looks to his father as his model.

In shifting allegiance toward his father, the boy asserts his right to be distinct and separate from his mother. Men and boys move away from, separate, push off, tumble, and roughhouse with other boys just like themselves. A boy develops in opposition to the mother who nourished him, but he is also drawn to women as a source of nourishment and sexual satisfaction, and that conflict is an eternal complication in his life: he might come to need the woman whose weakness he has rejected. Both men and women—everyone—yearn to return to that old warm union.

Everyone wishes at times to be the infant he once was, but that is forbidden to men when they leave the world of women. For if a boy relaxes his guard his mother will pull him into her again. This is not a conflict for girls, who physically continue an embedded life with the mother in their own bodies. According to May, women like to get closer, be part of, stay in touch with , and enjoy both the prospect and reality of having a baby grow inside them.

The emotional process that a patient, Richard, went through from his physical separation from his mother to his separation by divorce from his wife is an example of what many men experience. Richard began to pull away from his mother's kisses when he was about five, otherwise she would have smothered him. He really did not mean to hurt her feelings, but sometimes he wondered whether she got mad at him for slipping out of her arms and darting away. Maybe it was her idea in the first place that he was too old to climb onto her lap; maybe she thought he was turning into a mama's boy. The question he must answer for himself, then, is whether he has left his mother on his own or whether she forced him to go. One route is a free and manly one, the other is wimpy and weak, and that cannot be who he is. Even so, he cannot escape the question, because of what it might say about him. Perhaps he hurt his mother's feelings by wriggling around on her lap (he would not want to do that); or maybe it was the other way around and she pushed him out the door. If that was the case, then he was right to shrug her off.

While Richard was married and things went well, these worries were on hold. With the divorce they came up again. Richard thinks that while it is true that he left his wife, she may have pushed him out. To him, only a wimp would stay where he is not wanted, and only a wimp would let himself get pushed out without a fight. The matter of whether the husband jumped or was pushed is a current theme with an old history. The man likes to think that he left on his own, but when he doubts that conclusion, he feels small. In losing his marriage, Richard also lost the certainty that he was as strong and assertive as other men.

According to May, marriage, when it works, helps both partners to feel wanted because of the division of labor and the proud feeling of each person pulling their own weight. Also, women have a biological incentive to ride out the storms of marriage. For a man, each sexual act is a single experience, but for a woman each sexual act is a potential commitment that she will carry a baby for nine months and afterward find a sheltered place in which to raise that child. Those needs provide additional ballast for a woman; it is up to them to make the marriage endure. For example, although married women today work outside the home almost as much as their husbands do, the primary responsibility for running the house and child care remains in their hands, even though they may complain about it. A man may test his wife in some way—by spending a lot of time with his friends, for instance. On the woman's side, for her own (ultimate) biological aim, she will instinctively give him room. In accepting his behavior, she helps the man answer the question of whether his mother was trying to force him away, and for the time being he is satisfied that the answer is no.

Marriage also reassures the man that his strength benefits the family and contains his aggression in a way that pleases everyone. He builds and fixes and plants; he goes forth to make money. He is the most important man at home, without competition from his father or brothers, and he in turn puts his new family first. He is independent, ambitious, proud, competitive at work and sport, and sexually competent. He is a chip off the old block, and thus his boyhood values are confirmed. Figuratively speaking, he moves out and away from his wife in dealing with the world, reining himself in at his own pace. If he can regulate his movements, if he is always in charge, it will help him to feel autonomous, and from his side at least, the marriage will not be in danger.

Still, he does not let down his guard. Unconsciously, he is always negotiating for a comfortable distance between himself and his wife, and he is sensitive to pressure. She may become shrill when they argue an issue, and that feels like an attack. She may try to wrap him around her little finger or "get on his case." All this feels too hot, too sticky, and too close for the man's comfort. To save her feelings, he tunes her out and hopes she gets the message. If she continues to nag or make demands or tries to mother him, he will not make a fuss about it, because men simply do not do such things. He will move away from her a little in his mind and keep an eye on her. One thing is for sure: he is not going to let her make him feel small. It is bad enough that he has to hustle for respect at work; he is not going to put up with being pushed around at home. In a nice way, he tries to teach her a little something about boundaries: the rules and laws that men have lived by over the centuries to keep the peace. Marriage is no different. You do not have to raise your voice. Just follow the rules.

When Men Leave

Research indicates that many men leave for good when they feel devalued as lovers or moneymakers or as the head of the house. They leave because they are shamed in front of others, including children, friends, and in-laws. They leave for issues of prickly self-esteem and whenever they cannot make space for themselves. "I need more space," is familiar shorthand for a familiar issue, a replay of an old issue with the man's mother: boundaries and emotional temperature.

His wife is too close or too far, and the marriage is too cold or too hot. He feels suffocated or swallowed up. She is on his back or in his face, but sometimes she is an iceberg. Since many women tend to press for closeness to ensure that their mates will not abandon them and the children and since such men withdraw from closeness, the man may feel panicky when his wife comes too close. Still, her being too far away is, well, too far. It makes him look small in front of others if she does not stay somewhere close at hand.

Social situations must be open-ended so that he does not feel controlled; on the other hand, if there is no schedule or order in the house, it makes him look bad. Rather than leave his wife, he will try to regulate the distance in his own way, perhaps by working harder and longer at his job, working out at a gym, volunteering in the community, coaching a team, going drinking with other men, or changing his mind about having that couple she likes so much from the kids' school come for dinner.

To a man with such values, all these maneuvers are designed to do two things: reduce his anger at her cloying closeness, and save the marriage. He may have an affair at the office. The affair is meant to put even more distance between himself and his wife, to dilute the closeness between them without having to leave her. At best, however, he only dimly understands this. His wife is so totally outraged at his behavior when she learns about his affair that it always backfires. Then it is most shaming for him that his efforts have failed and that he cannot get through to his wife. He only wanted to come and go as a man must, but somehow she never got the message.

Social Forces

We are in the midst of a cultural transformation that has changed modern attitudes toward divorce. James Wilson states, "Cultural shift has as its central feature the emancipation of the individual from the restraints of tradition, community and government." This trend is worldwide. As a result, family bonds are weaker, and people are more careless about their obligations. The norm for the underclass, which is now spreading to the middle class, as are slovenly behavior and boom boxes, is for men to father a baby and leave. Sex has been divorced from commitment, and child rearing is separate from family life.

There is now a large group of young men who have dropped out of the labor force, ignore paternal responsibilities, and are part of an oppositional culture. Until 1980, increases in welfare benefits seemed to explain the continuing rise in illegitimacy. Since then welfare benefits have increased little, but the increase in illegitimate births has continued. Today, one out of three children is born out of wedlock. For some, fathering children has become a rite of passage.

Policymakers like Wilson feel that it is crucial to change the behavior of fathers who do not live up to their child support responsibilities by making failure to pay child support a crime and tracking these delinquent fathers through drivers' and professional licenses.

No Reward for Good Behavior

The struggling, harassed working father heading for divorce has nothing but disgust for the unemployed male who deserts his baby at birth. Even so he cannot help noticing that that father has succeeded in taking off and escaping blame because the government takes care of the mother and child. The divorcing father says to himself, there is no reward for good behavior. He has been trying to do the right thing for everyone in the family for years, yet still they are hostile and blaming. Meanwhile, the boy who fathered a baby is long gone; no one calls him to account.

It does seem that the erosion of commitment is spreading. Only half of all divorced men pay the full amount agreed to for child support; 25 percent do not pay anything; the other 25 percent pay erratically. Susan Faludi states in her book *Backlash* that divorced men are now more likely to meet their car payments than their child support obligations. Some fathers do not pay out of vengeance, because the other parent has custody of the children and the day-to-day pleasure of their company. Sometimes the father does not pay because his ex-wife will not work; others because it hurts their pride to be ordered by the court or anyone else to do something; or because the father remarries and has a baby, and the new family emotionally replaces the former one.

Incest and Accusations of Incest

Both sides use custody fights as forms of emotional blackmail, and in any given year there are many thousands of kidnappings by one parent or the other. To break a murderous deadlock, one parent or the other will escalate the charges and push for a rift that cannot be repaired. Abduction is one sure way to do it; a charge of child abuse is another. In either case, all negotiation is over between the couple, and the case then becomes one for the courts and child development experts.

When a mother accuses the father of sexually molesting the child while the child is visiting him, the nature of the cutoff escalates with the perceived nature of the crime: the mother and child may go into hiding; the child may be hidden away in another state, and the mother goes to jail; or the child may be abducted by either parent. These apocalyptic battles have their beginnings in ordinary marital warfare. In a deteriorating marriage, using children to score points is the surest way to ensure that the "bad" parent is out of the child's life. For example, in order to get custody, Edwin monitored his ex-wife closely and had her followed whenever she went out. He said in court that Marion was dangerous to the children because she was an alcoholic who was careless about safety when drunk. She came home from a bar one night, he explained, and left the garage door open. After the divorce, when the mother got custody, she wanted an increase in child support so that she could go into family therapy with the children, who were traumatized by the father's accusations. The father then reported that the younger boy had suspicious bruises on his ribs; the mother countered by reporting that the five-year-old girl returned from a visit to her father with a vaginal discharge.

There is real child abuse, which is a horror, and then there is the cynical accusation of it after divorce, when the family system is flooded with aggression and the only relief is murder or cutoff. In this story and others, it will take years to disentangle the charges and counter charges. Meanwhile, the family is moving toward cutoff, although it is not yet clear which family member will be ejected. Because of media reports, the father increasingly believes that he will be singled out, and that also influences him to cut off before he is targeted.

Worn down and exhausted, people look for a way out. The same behavior they once labeled irresponsible they now see as their only hope. Furthermore, getting out and starting over seem sanctioned by both the inherited values of the American West and the street values that have slipped into the mainstream. The underclass, formed in aggression, will not take on middle-class values. Middle-class parents, worn down by aggression, *will* adopt the more accepting street values because aggression seems to be the only potent weapon against aggression. (In the United States we know this because of the escalation of violence at every level of our society.)

Some fathers show their frustration over their demeaned life by angry withdrawal as well as violence, although at first glance this is surprising because economically they come out well ahead of their ex-wives. According to Wallerstein and Blakeslee, their income increases by 42 percent, while women experience a steep decline in their standard of living during the same period. Women are often stressed to the breaking point as well, owing to increased responsibilities coupled with a lowered income. A two-tiered society, with women and children as an underclass that includes divorced women, middle-class women, and women from the ghetto and working class, seems to be an existing reality.

Why do mothers who have custody of their children not desert their families in greater numbers? Although they are poorer and struggle harder after divorce, the difference is probably that they have not lost their children, and keeping the family structure saves their morale. After divorce, fathers who lose custody come out worse in the most difficult task of all, which is to disentangle themselves from being half of a couple while remaining a parent. Those who lose this struggle during the transition do so because they have no structure to see them through it.

Such a displaced father is looking for a new place, yes, but he is also in emotional limbo. In modern marriage, the distinctions between parenting and child rearing are blurred, but after divorce it takes each parent several years to make a transition to a new position: mother-on-her-own, father-on-his-own. Without a solid base, the emotional passage is too difficult. It is also exhausting, shaming, and unfair: Even if the father always put his children first. In most divorces he loses them and somehow loses his place in the community as well.

Many middle-class women today are proud of being single parents and brag that they can make it on their own. Some feel they do not need a man in their lives; in other cases the baby can come from a sperm bank and never know its father. In the ghetto, as well as out of it, there are those who father children and go—and this pattern seems to be escalating. To a greater or less extent, then, in considering what contributes to fathers' leaving, we must add to the list the temper of the times.

7

PARENTS
AND CHILDREN
AFTER DIVORCE

There are three sure products of divorce: rage, worry about the children, and limited hope for the future. Can they ever be reconciled?

Rage

The rage after divorce is inevitable: everything familiar is gone and yet, more than ever, arrangements for the future depend on the estranged spouse: the one who left you or the one you could not wait to leave. "She wanted me gone," one husband said bitterly, "but divorce with kids has a half-life all its own, and we're stuck with each other forever." In the act of disengagement, the old ties are inevitably confusing and must be worked through one by one. It takes extraordinary determination just to get through the process.

In the unraveling, all the emotions wound: envy, hatred, a burning desire for revenge, feelings of abandonment, fear, and loneliness. There are no tender feelings here. At various times in the process, divorce makes each spouse feel helpless, and when one feels helpless, tears only make it worse. Rage is the one empowering emotion left. One elderly woman went across town in a snowstorm to slash her husband's tires. Rage also overcomes ambivalence, and when the new enemy has also been the old lover, there is always ambivalence.

Most couples who ultimately divorce drag on uncertainly together for months or years before taking the final step, adding to the tension of a divorce in the making and causing everyone to strike out in fury. During this period more than half the children of divorcing parents, children who had never witnessed any violence at all, see their parents hit each other for the first time. Rage overcomes ambivalence, all right, but, paradoxically, while it is being enacted, rage ties the divorcing couple together long and hard, and there is no room for anything else. For example, in the first year or two after divorce, fathers establish relationships with their children that pretty much remain the same. Follow-up studies show that when negotiations with ex-wives are stormy, fathers are less involved with their children later: either their interest wanes or they cut off altogether. If parents were aware that they set the tone for years to come during the divorce itself, they might be motivated to devise a way to bind or redirect their anger in order to prevent a catastrophic fallout for the children. The emphasis in a first mediating session, for example, might be the connection between continuing marital warfare and the father's cutoff from the children.

Cutting Off is Easier Than Connecting

There are many reasons why rage is the preferred emotion of divorce: rage demonstrates the frustration of (often inexpressible) feelings most clearly. Divorce itself is enraging; no matter who did what to whom, each party feels abandoned by the other, and until the eleventh hour each is convinced that the other will reclaim him or her. When that fails to happen, there is disbelief —and there is rage. Also, rage is enlivening and single-minded, while sadness and yearning and love for the one you have lost only make you want to die.

Above all, rage is the road to cutoff. Rage is the preferred emotion because it overcomes ambivalence. When the divorcing couple was still in love, they tolerated the ambivalence between them for the sake of continuing the relationship (and all relationships are ambivalent). Now that they are adversaries, the ambivalence is intolerable, and they must not be ambivalent; they must get out.

As we know, anger is also an early stage of mourning, and the later stages are even more wrenching, and so, unconsciously, rage is often used to abort mourning. After a parent's death, for example, brothers and sisters get caught up in wrangles about property. These fights poison the air for years and displace the mourning for the dead parent. They also serve as a cover for old rivalries between siblings that the parents had held in check. The brothers and sisters then go on together, smoldering, angrily dependent on their continuing grievance; or they cut off. In either case they have aborted the bewildering upsurge of emotions that is such a frightening part of mourning. Anger overtakes loss. In divorce, also, frozen rage keeps the couple angrily dependent on each other and prevents them from moving on more happily with someone else.

If a couple continues to be angry after divorce, that style of relating affects all new relationships, including those with new spouses. New marriages are happier when the preceding divorce went well, and it is not hard to understand why: the anger still invested in an old marriage hangs over the new one.

Even so, no one grieves willingly; grief is awful and isolating, a lonely state of consciousness. Those who have truly loved are absorbed into the grieving process as though unconsciously paying the price for having loved. Those who truly hate are absolved from it, and this is the goal that partners in bad marriages strive for: a rage that will set them free. Sue Hubbell, the nature writer, tells the story of her grandmother, a timid, sad-faced woman who regained her spirit after her husband's death and outlived him by many years. "Toward the end of her life, she gathered her grandchildren around her. 'I want you to remember your grandfather, always,' she said. We nodded solemnly. She beckoned us closer. 'I want you to remember that he was a mean, dirty, stingy old man,' she said in a firm voice and then looked off into the distance, a pleased smile playing over her lips." This partner, for one, was sure of her feelings, but most endings are ambivalent. The brothers and sisters who fight over property after their parents' death hate each other but also have some good, loving memories—if and when they will allow them to surface. They also have remorse and resentment about who did or did not take care of the parents in their last days. Without a sifting, observing, and working through, these losses remain unresolved.

Divorce: The Death That Will Not Die

Divorce feels like death but is not death and cannot be put to rest, because the "dead" one keeps making trouble. People are also frustrated because they have lost a mate who will not die. There is no loving closure and no place in the psychic memory bank for one who is gone but not gone, and so a place must be created. If the grieving process goes forward, it takes about two years to put a divorce to rest, but some people cannot tolerate anguish for this long, and they displace the anger of the mourning process itself onto a living family member. At first the anger is locked between the divorcing couple, then it spills over to the children.

Because divorce has a dubious status to begin with (the couple had other options, after all), no one notices that the two partners are stuck in misery, and so "divorce" and "mourning" are not usually mentioned together. This attitude is reflected in the fact that divorce is the only major family crisis in which outsiders are reluctant to help. Friends are afraid that they will have to take sides; neighbors think it is none of their business; family are discomfited. The world believes what each divorcing spouse secretly believes: "If only I had tried harder," the marriage could have been saved. Although half of the sixty families in the Wallerstein and Blakeslee study belonged to churches or synagogues, not one member of the clergy called on the adults or children during the divorce.

Preparing For Divorce

The indifference of outsiders, however, is frequently inadvertent. Some people who are awkward about coming forward on their own are relieved when asked to help; once their consciousness has been raised, they are more obliging.

Competence dilutes rage, and either parent will feel less guilty and less frazzled about the children—less enraged—if he or she has provided warm and reliable stand-ins. (And for the moment, the feeling of helplessness will go.) It is a little like packing your bag and making all the necessary calls before you go to the hospital: you can take better care of yourself after you have arranged for the care of those who matter to you.

These arrangements are easier for women to act on than for men because women are used to asking for and giving help. Many women willingly go to clinical psychologists and social workers when they are in trouble. Few men will. A man with a broken part will go to a doctor and have it fixed, but that is true of broken parts only, not broken hearts. For many men, tender feelings come perilously close to weakness and can be shown only obliquely, as in gratitude for the doctor who cures them, for example. For these men, only anger can be expressed directly.

As a result, men have no easy way to express themselves to themselves when their deepest feelings are tapped; they can only despise themselves when they let themselves down. The trouble with advising divorced fathers to call on others for help is that many men find the very idea of asking for support humiliating. They do not even know how to ask; their emotions are imprisoned. Rage is such a man's refuge because sadness is immobilizing, fragmenting, and "soft." It is unlike a man to talk to a therapist or a friend, but alone he can express himself productively by "making" something: keeping a journal, woodworking, or painting. This way, as a first step, he can express himself to himself in private. After a while, and again in private, he may be able to revisit some of his imprisoned feelings. The keeping of a journal, for example, helps to elaborate feelings for oneself, and a man can think about his feelings at leisure.

Creating something new (a product or a change in consciousness) helps to center one without calling on another person. The relaxed rhythm of these activities is very different from the unforgiving pace of everyday life, but each involves a making of something all the same.

All these activities lead to the self-mastery men have known since they became self-conscious but which they forget under stress.

The Language of Emotional Negotiation

One of the major reasons why some men divorce their children as well as their wives is connected to these self-imposed strictures, that is, they have no language for the negotiation of emotional issues. Men are better at doing and making than they are at talking. For a good, functional negotiation, everyone involved must work with this difference between the sexes. It is just a difference, not a crime. For example, after divorce, paternal grandparents are usually less involved with their grandchildren than they were before. Whether they remain in contact depends on two factors: (1) whether their son still sees the children, and (2) whether their daughter-in-law keeps in touch with them. If it is hard for a man to express himself to himself, it will be hard for him to have the language necessary to speak to his parents.

An accepted part of these same findings about men and their parents is that, as C.A. Ahrons states, "Some in-laws cannot accept two affiliations and may shift loyalty from the first spouse to the second." This assertion lacks credibility, for grandparents parent whether they have one child or ten, and they grandparent in the same way. It is more likely that the son does not want to talk about the divorce and that the grandparents do not know how to ask about it. The son's parents notice that he is working too hard or smoking too much or making frenzied arrangements to date, and they do not want to add to his unhappiness by asking difficult questions. Failing to speak about what is under everyone's nose, however, adds to the tension over it. A situation that is just plain bad is then also made to feel shameful. Shame and silence increase when the son stops seeing his children altogether, and as time passes it is harder to intervene.

One of the many games people play as divorce negotiations drag on is to withhold visitation from one side or the other until there is so much bad feeling toward the in-law parent that the children are forgotten. The grandparents are frustrated, baffled, and injured by their son's troubles and protest this blow to him by hurting their daughter-in-law. Their son, by his silence, seems to condone the cutoff, and maybe he does. It is not always collusion, however; sometimes it is simply ineptness. Cutting off from the children is the most potent form of protest there is: it does indeed punish the daughter-in-law. Even so, no one on the noncustodial side might choose this form of protest should an alternative present itself.

In the novel *The Unbearable Lightness of Being*, by the Czech writer Milos Kundera, the hero, Tomas, cuts off from his child after divorce because his ex-wife is arbitrary about his visiting rights. In retaliation for refusing to see his son, Tomas's own parents cut off from him. Yet he has no remorse; he continues to pay child support but remains aloof. His pride is better served by not being made to feel helpless than by any connection to his parents or son.

How to Make the Transition: What Might Work

In a divorce in which the woman is sole custodial parent, the paternal side of the family is most vulnerable to a cutoff during the transition from father-and-husband to father-on-his-own. While negotiating with his wife about his old life, the husband has to remake his life to include the children in a new way and in a new place. Emotionally he is moving away from his former wife in his mind at the same time that he is trying to get closer to their children. He may act out this heightened conflict when they are all together. He may have had a fight with his ex-wife at the very moment that the children run in smiling and saying hello. It is all very confusing, enraging, and exhausting. He knows that he has to keep some connection to his former wife, whom he now hates, but how on earth will he know which ties to break and which ones are important to the children?

There is no ritual for this legal and social change; it is often overlooked by such divorce professionals as lawyers, therapists, and mediators simply because such sessions are already jam-packed with other issues. Yet even for the couple mediating on its own, calling a nameless fear by name reduces anxiety.

"We're meeting today to talk about the best living arrangements for the children. It's a new way to talk, so we've all agreed to a time limit. Undoing a marriage can feel scary even when you do it a little at a time, so don't be hard on yourself if you feel upset. We will try to keep it short."

This way of opening a meeting is a small ritual, signaling change in an acceptable way. It calls attention to the task—the transition and its difficulties—acknowledges anxiety and fear, and tries to free the couple from blaming themselves or others. It also calls on the participants to observe what they themselves are doing. If they can stand away from themselves a little during a difficult transaction it will help to increase emotional distance in the long run; as emotional distance increases, a natural boundary forms between marriage and parenting.

Change, entry, and reentry—all kinds of difficult transitions—are all made easier if they are respectfully marked. When no acknowledgment was forthcoming for one ten-year-old who lives with one family one week and with another family the next week, she suggested that each family make the transitions easier by telling her a little about what happened while she was gone. This wise child reminded her elders that entry and reentry were a large part of her life. This is indeed the case in divorce and makes all the difference to people, whether child or parent, who do not quite know where they fit in the family anymore.

Sandy and Herb

It also helps if a couple can make transitional arrangements themselves before a divorce is final. They can set the tone. While their divorce was in progress, Sandy offered her husband the use of their house to see the children until he had a place of his own. She thought about putting a limit on the time he could use it but decided that she was more interested in providing a regular place for the children to be with their father than in making points. She did not forget that their relationship was changing, though, and made a note to work out this new boundary with Herb as part of their shared custody agreement.

Herb then initiated what came to be part of a transitional ritual between them that helped to make the divorce less onerous. Like a polite guest he said, "Oh, there you are, Sandy. We've had a good time, but the children missed you, so I'll just kiss them goodbye for now." When he arrived the next time, Sandy took up the cue and said, "Here you are, Herb. The kids are ready and waiting, and I'll get out. Would you give Derek a baby aspirin at four, please? Thanks."

Sandy and Herb were working out a contract to be partners in parenting, which shifts the issue from marriage to their joint concern for the children, a goal that is outside each partner. Their transitional behavior already reflects that shift. If the couple can use the shift to work through other issues before their divorce is final, they will feel less victimized by the process. Their behavior now is a good model for each of them: the more each spouse takes charge of what he or she can take charge of, the better each will feel.

Distance

Sandy and Herb have begun the process of "a good divorce" through a change of demeanor. Deliberate distancing (as in writing) is another kind of change, appropriate to divorce and different from the hostile distance that has brought the couple to divorce in the first place. They find themselves divorcing because they did not recognize the distancing maneuvers that each used during the marriage. At the time they called it "his" moodiness or "her" need to spend more time with her sister, but it was really a signal that the boundaries between them did not feel right to one or the other. Similarly, when the divorcing process derails, people send the wrong clues about what they want, and the protracted marital wars that ensue become a new form of emotional dependency. In other words, the same issues that were left unresolved in the marriage—boundaries, intimacy, how hot, how cold, the good and bad uses of dependency—resurface in the divorce and paralyze it. In the following vignette, the couple tried in good faith to make adjustments in their marriage that would take the other's needs into account, but they faltered because they could not quite locate or name the problem, which was negotiating boundaries. Paradoxically, they were better at it after their divorce.

John and Holly

John was a loner who concentrated on school. He immersed himself in computers, got a doctorate in computer science, and found a good technical and administrative job at a bank. He worked well by himself but was not forthcoming with others; he would work overtime rather than go to the trouble of explaining the work to a co-worker. He had a natural ability for soccer, but team sports made him uncomfortable; he preferred running. He was shy and correct in company and went out infrequently, but in his thirties he was captivated by a bubbling young woman, a teacher, whom he met on a hiking trip. She had many interests and did not especially mind when John worked late, even after they were married. After their first child was born he seemed to work even later, and Holly wondered uneasily whether John preferred working to being with her and their son. She put it out of her mind because he was otherwise so agreeable. Although he generally went along amiably with anything she proposed, Holly noticed that he withdrew silently when he had had enough—when people began to chit-chat after a zoning board meeting at their house, for example, or after a concert at the university.

Holly loved being a mother and wanted a second child; she did not mind the idea of raising a baby on her own if John continued to work late. She was surprised when he protested. He said that he preferred a quiet life, that the apartment was already too noisy, and little Teddy jumped around too much and needed attention. This shocked her. "He's a three-year old. They jump around. That is their job description!" But Holly was also practical and sensible. She put up thick drapes for insulation against the noise in the street, realizing that John, like her three-year-old, needed more quiet time. She kept Teddy's record player off when John was home and arranged for John to read to his son or build with blocks and Tinker Toys. If Teddy whined, however, it seemed to unnerve John, and Holly took him away.

When Emily was born, John said that he could not stand the bustle and the crying at night, the boom boxes in the street, and the feeling that his life was being run by other people. He left the house to live on his own when Emily was three months old and colicky.

John got an apartment in a quiet neighborhood close to the university and regularly visited the children. In his restrained way, he seemed to enjoy being with them at the time but rarely asked for more time. He wrote notes to Holly on household matters through e-mail. He also gave her computer copies of the visiting schedule, revised as necessary. The schedule made clear what was expected of anyone at any time; John liked limits and structure and hated surprises. If a change was due, he wanted to be warned about it two weeks in advance so that he could adjust to it. He took the children to a museum or library when he had extra time with them, which, Holly noticed, became a little boring for them. She asked John whether he would think about getting Teddy a bicycle and teach him to ride it.

"When would I do that?"

"Whenever it works out for you."

"You mean as long as it's not raining or snowing?"

"Well, yes. But there's no rush. Just think about it."

"I'll think about it," John agreed, adding, "Teddy's getting tall fast. In a little while I'm going to teach him to shoot baskets, too."

He remembered Holly's zoning board meetings and her reading group nights, although she did not put them on the schedule, and offered to sit. Holly sometimes agreed but felt uneasy if she and John were too friendly. She never wanted the divorce in the first place, and it made her angry that he worked out such a cozy divorce. It probably scared him, too. They had sex once or twice postdivorce, and it was too close for him, she thought, as he was a little cool toward her for a time. Holly began to date, which John did not know, and wanted to marry again; that would help to make their boundaries clearer. "If we were a couple without children it might have worked, but not with children. They're too lively and too unpredictable."

Holly said that before she married John there were all kinds of warning signs telling her not to get too close to him, but she believes she was willfully blind because she wanted children. John sometimes had tantrums when there were too many changes, such as moving or traveling. If there were too many people in the house, he withdrew. When he came home from work, he used to ring or knock, which was irritating, even though he had his own key. "I mean, he made a boundary wherever he could, but did I see it? No, I didn't. He used to say, 'I need my own cubicle,' and I knew what he was talking about, but we liked each other, and so we just crossed our fingers and hoped it would get warmer. Anyway, if that's the choice, marriage or divorce with children, I know I would be miserable without the kids." She also became tolerant of his choice. "He helped me to understand him," she says, "because he knew what he was like, and he didn't want to run out on us."

He had to leave the house because the emotional "neediness" of his family, as he called it, felt foreign to him. In their presence, he constantly felt he was a failure. He was awkward and stiff when he comforted the children and could not engage in spontaneous play; he could not anticipate what they needed, and it seemed to him undignified to try.

John came from a silent farm family that showed their fondness for each other by pitching in with any task that needed doing without being asked. They did not ask any questions (they thought it intrusive); they never made personal comments (they thought it was impolite); and they were stoic about all disappointments, from the death of a farm animal or a drought to the long-term illness and death of a family member (they hated a fuss.) John was like them: responsible but remote. Emotional display was so foreign to him that when Holly laughed, cried, or raised her voice, it felt like a direct assault. The shouts and cries of his own small children amplified that effect, he was ashamed to say. He was also a little embarrassed when the children ran around in circles and fell down for the fun of it. Although he knew he could not ask it of them, he wished that Holly and the children could be more restrained. The following is from Holly:

> When I take the kids to the farm to visit his folks and his brother, they find it hard to make eye contact, and yet they'd do anything for us. They like us. They're just a very inhibited bunch. The kids don't seem to have inherited those genes, thank Heavens. I've had a lot of time to think about it, and even John gets better at understanding what happened. It seems to be a combination of temperament and shame. Whatever it is, I've come to think that the lucky thing about John is that even though emotion terrifies him, he was the first to recognize the warning signs. When we had children he knew that if he did not figure out how to make a space, he would run out on us altogether.
>
> Well, he's really not built that way; he would never run out, but he's sensitive in a way I had to learn—it's so foreign to me. John is sensitive to overstimulation, noise, boundaries. Let's see, what else? He's ashamed of not being spontaneous, but he

falls apart if he doesn't have control over every single detail because he's afraid of making a fool of himself. So that makes him very self-conscious. What else? Let's see . . . jealous at not getting the attention the children get but hating himself for it because he should be bigger than that, and a good person should not think of himself at all. Well, I could go on, but at least he noticed these things about himself and did something about them. There are many men in this neighborhood who have these same issues to some degree, but I don't think they ever figured it out, and I'm talking about these smart university types—physicists and medical researchers—and some of them are long gone. The only thing that saves this awful situation in our case is that John has a conscience. If I give him lots and lots of space, he'll always come through for me and the kids.

Worry About the Children

Most couples work out custody arrangements on their own. In San Mateo County, California, for example, only fourteen out of one thousand custody cases had to be decided by a judge. Holly had physical custody, but she and John had flexible visiting arrangements. Even though John preferred visiting the children at Holly's apartment, joint custody was a vote of confidence for John that will enable him to widen his contact with the children as they grow.

These days, women's organizations are much less enthusiastic about joint custody than when it first became popular in the 1980s, because the father with his own household cuts down on the child support he pays, often leaving the ex-wife beleaguered with bills. The wife is often bitterly double-bound: fathers divorce their children as well as their wives because they do not feel like fathers anymore owing to the loss of family structure. Two real households is obviously the answer, but that solution also causes new, conflicting problems for the woman since joint custody probably means less money.

Sharing custody is an emotional sacrifice for her because, as hard as it is to raise children alone, it is harder to feel that they may come to prefer the other parent. Even so, she will probably agree because, as studies show, the most involved father is a joint-custody parent who is satisfied with the custody decision. Studies also show that in most cases he is single, as is his ex-spouse, and has a better-than-average education. He is in frequent touch with his family, and both parents are supportive of the other's relationship with the child. The separate parents do not allow their conflicts to interfere with parenting. The joint-custody father feels satisfied with his role in the child's life and has better relations with his ex-wife than the father who distances himself. If he has remarried, amicable relations between the first and second wife help. According to Ahrons, under these conditions, the father is likely to remain in his child's life and to continue child support.

The Reality Principal

The complicated arrangements that people make for their children after divorce are a reminder that somehow, after the bitter early stages, most divorced couples are capable of compromise and negotiation. But how do the rage, reluctance, and avoidance of early divorce become transformed into a workable relationship? How can it be that a couple who have worn each other down for years with demands and counterdemands can still come together in an altruistic way in the best interest of the child?

The pleasure in rage is gradually replaced by the pressures and pleasures of real life. Time, distance, and new pursuits help the couple to go beyond rage toward a more rational appraisal of the needs of the children. Moore and Fine, in *A Glossary of Psychoanalitic Terms and Concepts*, state that "The change from being ruled by the pleasure principle to the more restrained and rational forms of thought, feelings and action characteristic of the reality principle, involves delays, postponements, renunciations and other more complex inhibitions." These words, which define the reality principle in psychoanalytic terms, might have been designed especially for those who have come through the crucible of divorce. These adults, now experienced in ways they never hoped to be, have accepted the "delays, postponements, renunciations and other complex inhibitions" of divorce and for their pains have gained a depth of understanding that will carry them through other trials. Meanwhile, owing to the grueling efforts of the parents, their children will have two parents.

What it Takes to Make it Work

In the current divorce judgments men are usually the non-custodial parent. These men divorce their children as well as their wives out of a cumulative sense of injury that is inflamed by the process of divorce itself. They have lost everything and yet have to continue to pay (double jeopardy). At all points of transition, entry, and reentry they feel small and devalued. They think it is weak to feel bad or talk to anyone about feeling bad, so they have only a couple of ways to adapt—fight or flight. After the fight is lost (as they believe), they flee. Palliatives will not help, because the sense of injury is too great. Although we can get men to pay child support by enacting tougher laws, the long-term damage to children without fathers is an issue the law cannot affect.

The best way to prevent men such as those from leaving their children is to be aware of their deep feelings of injury and to be sensitive in response. This may seem like giving men more than they deserve for a duty that women perform willingly and at great sacrifice, but the fact is that when men feel shamed and see no way out, they leave. When they feel that they have lost the fight, they go. These are the major areas of injury that cause lingering resentment in a man:

First, the loss of daily contact with his children, the loss of family life, and the large outlays of money.

Second, when the marriage breaks up, he looks like the bad guy to all the world because he is the one who leaves the house. Meanwhile, it is his life that is shattered; he, not she, must invent a new way to be with the children, while his own life arrangements are ramshackle or temporary.

Third, the children become adversaries too. More and more, they echo his wife's constant demands on him, and after a while he cannot tell whether she put them up to it or not. In any case, he cannot quite trust them.

Fourth, the children also remind him of the uneasy feelings he suppressed when they were born. When each one came, his wife was more obsessed with the baby than she had ever been with him. He lost her as friend and sexual partner for months at a time, and he lost the exclusive relationship he had with her for all time. He was getting nothing then, and he noticed that she was getting just about everything she wanted: talking baby talk to the baby as though she were the baby herself and attending to it day and night as though she were the only mother on earth. He was cheerful and helpful at the time despite these feelings; he knew they were petty but could not quite dismiss them. Still, it was an unpleasant reminder to him of life with his own mother; once again he had been pushed aside.

Fifth, in divorce, old feelings of deprivation return: again the father has to pay and pay again for his wife's closeness to the children, even as he loses her and them, and the subliminal feeling that the children are responsible for the breakup between the couple takes hold in spite of himself.

Sixth, with everything going out and nothing coming in, the broken connection to his children—a life of interruption and nervous waiting—is too hard to take. Every time he sees the children he is reminded of loss. His wife has emptied him out, filled herself with his children and his goods, and left him with nothing.

Finally, therefore, he cuts off because his grief cannot be resolved; he is always being reintroduced to loss and envy.

Hope for the Future

Although the same may be said for women in similar straits who abandon their families, it is, by current standards, most frequently men who leave. In this situation, when a man leaves his family in a way that shames him—if he has been abusive or unfaithful, a gambler or a bankrupt—he may think that he is doing the children a favor by getting out of their lives. It may even be true at the time. When his life changes, he may still hesitate to reconnect, afraid of opening up all the old wounds, his and theirs. The children remind him of the person he was at the time of the divorce, he does not like that person anymore, and neither do the children, and so he finds new reasons to distance himself from them.

Jerry

This was the case with Jerry, a divorced father, when he came back to the United States after two years in South America. During that time he had not seen his three children at all. Jerry was a successful entrepreneur with a heavy cocaine habit whose work was staging outdoor extravaganzas. The children were a year apart. When the oldest child was entering her teens, his wife found it untenable to cover up for Jerry's drug habit anymore and filed for divorce. Jerry went on a bender after the final decree and lost track of his family for more than a year in a maze of drug and business deals but gradually pulled himself together. While in South America and on drugs he had tried to stage an animal ballet, starring baby llamas, and this episode had landed him on the front page of his local suburban paper, where the drugs were highly featured. The children cut off from him altogether. Fran felt vindicated in having divorced him—he had proved himself an idiot and a fool—and did not support his efforts to reconnect with his children.

Jerry persisted and kept in contact with them all by phone, letter, and e-mail. After a lapse, his child support became more regular. When he wrote to the children, he often closed with the lines, "I wasn't much good to you the last few years, but try me now," although he could never bring himself to say anything like that over the phone. When his middle child failed to show up for a birthday dinner his father had for him, Jerry sent him the present with the note, "Sorry we missed each other."

Fran was not hostile anymore; she was not friendly either. She was more or less bemused at Jerry's persistence after his disgrace and long absence. By the time they had been divorced for two and a half years, she had a new boyfriend. The children waited for Jerry's calls—Christmas, their birthdays, the Fourth of July. Would he set off firecrackers? Would he call with some kind of crazy plan? He did. They watched and waited and had a pact between themselves never to initiate a call to him. Sometimes, when he trapped one of them on the phone and made a date, they acted out his old game of desertion and stood him up. He remained even-tempered.

Jerry was determined to square himself in his children's eyes and kept at it. His self-esteem was tied to being a good father, and he went at the project with wit and energy. One night he showed up unexpectedly at their high school for a basketball game and sat down beside them. Because they did not want to be embarrassed in front of their friends, the children went along with him afterward to a local restaurant. An old neighbor was there with his children, and Jerry, taking his son Robbie with him, went over to speak to the man. Jerry told Lou, the neighbor, that he had deserted the kids when they needed him but had seen the error of his ways through Narcotics Anonymous and hoped to make it up to them. Lou was a little embarrassed at the unexpected confession. Then he said, "But, Jerry, you were always fun!" and they made a tennis date. The children were furious but a little impressed, too, that their dad had not tried to hide why he had been away. Robbie said, "He was talking like a Holy Roller."

Jerry moved to the suburb where his ex-wife lived to be closer to the children. He joined the tennis club, and set up a high school tennis tournament. He also took the children back to an old neighborhood in the city where they had lived when they were small. He and the children reminisced about what they remembered from those days, the good and the bad. They sat in a little park near the old house, and according to the children, "We let him have it." All the hurt and quarreling before their parents had broken up and the postdivorce years when their father had left, came pouring out. They said that they had felt like freaks when he took off and that they often wished him dead "when you left us for dead."

He said, "I think you were right to want to kill me," and "Let's come here again. It seems like a good place to talk." They went to the little park in the old neighborhood several times and then began looking up old neighbors and playmates. Lisa, the only girl and the oldest, reconnected with an old friend and from that time on often came into the city to ice skate with her. The questions and recriminations did not end, but little by little they were letting their father back into their lives. For example, one son agreed to play in the tennis tournament his father organized.

Jerry had a plan to ground himself in his children and the family network to make sure "I never fly sky high again." He felt sure that intense devotion to these ideals would be his remaking and would also enrich his children's lives. This fierce conviction kept him going even when he was rebuffed. He had always wanted to visit odd pockets of his own family, cousins and second cousins, scattered around the country, and tried to interest the children in this plan. Finally, Lisa and his son Todd agreed to go. They drove around one summer introducing themselves. They all liked learning family history and were pleased by the physical resemblance and talents they found they had in common (two of the cousins were gifted musicians, as was Robbie). After that, the children, who had begun to go to college, planned a cousins' reunion for their father's side of the family; Robbie and his cousins would provide the music.

Jerry's mother and aunt had been timid about seeing the children while Jerry was not paying child support regularly, but he got them to reconnect and to go on family outings, and they all became even more firmly reconnected through the cousins' connection. Each of these connections seemed to strengthen the one between Jerry and the children, and, he felt, strengthened his feeling of having both feet on the ground.

The best and surest way he knew to rebuild his own life was to be a good father. That was the easy part. It was still hard for him to face the children's anger about his desertion. As it kept flaring up in one or the other child, it seemed insurmountable. They accused him of trying to buy off their bad memories with tennis, the old neighborhood, and trips to visit all his relatives: "the happy, happy family." It is true that he had left them in a spectacularly crazy way, pawning some valuable paintings and selling off joint stock and then flying to South America to buy and live on drugs. If they never wanted to see him again, who could blame them?

They kept up a steady drum beat of anger, bravura, and sulking fits, but sometimes Lisa would shyly kiss him, and the boys would lock arms with him. He did not understand it, but it kept him going. Yet just when he was beginning to feel a little more comfortable with them, either Lisa, Robbie, or Todd would take turns reminding him how their mother had to beg for money from her family when he was gone, how they felt like freaks at school, how kids left notes in their lockers asking them in Spanish if they wanted to buy Inca Gold. Jerry heard them out without defending himself. "I have no excuses for the past. It was bad. I can only keep trying now."

As there were three of them and any one of them could easily tyrannize the remaining child if one of them left the pack, all the children kept the testing going to make sure that they did not let their father off too easily. They had to keep showing him their anger until they were empty of it. Adolescent boys, especially, feel a growing need for their fathers and believe that the fathers are not closer to them because they, the children, are not good enough! While the children are thinking that they were not good enough to keep him, the father who left them keeps feeling that he is not good enough to return and will be rejected if he does. For father and children who have been separated by divorce, the years of absence are proof that they are all failures. When he does come back, the relationship has to be negotiated all over again.

Through this testing period, it helped that Jerry had spent his life in a business that required a thick skin, that he had the support of Narcotics Anonymous, that he was unusually energetic and inventive, and that he had a passion for details, and, strangely enough, that he was methodical. He took on the wooing of the children as a task that he must complete, the booking he must get, the spiritual journey that mattered. His persistence finally paid off. The children took him back. "But how did you do it?" someone asked him. "Well, when Robbie did not show up for his birthday, for instance, I just told myself, 'Oh yeah, and what about that time the elephants were late?'" Creative plans, a new way to be together, mark a transition to a good postdivorce relationship.

8

AN ABSOLUTE NEED TO CUT OFF: INCEST OR "INCEST"

"I was one of those who accused my innocent father."
—Melody Gavigan, *The Retractors' Newsletter*

Melody Gavigan is a retractor, someone who has charged another family member with sexual abuse and later says that the accusation was untrue. Sex and violence are the major themes of the 1990s. Incest has always been a form of violence—a violating use of sex—and incest universally repels us. "Incest," as a false memory, uses the protective coloration of true incest to the same effect; it is a camouflage that always works since no family can survive the accusation of incest unscathed, whether or not it is true.

Although experts themselves can hardly distinguish between real and false claims of incest, one difference seems to be that women who have been molested as children can usually recall some of the details of the experience: "My uncle grabbed me just as everyone was going to the door after my eighth birthday party and stuck his tongue in my mouth."

For those who retrieve memories of incest or abuse for the first time as adults, memory starts as a vague feeling that is then embellished in each retelling and often grows to a full-scale narrative. Yet even then it is never done: retrieved memories continue to breed new ones. Those who retrieve memories as adults are also more likely to use those memories as a way out of the family, a way to cut off.

The question that is the hardest to answer is, why would anyone go to such lengths to cut off when there has been no abuse of any kind? The answer seems to be that the themes supplied by our times—sex and violence—are the very ones needed to justify an absolute cutoff that no one can question. False incest suits the zeitgeist of our society in every way. It also suits a psychological need to sever ties completely: there must be a psychological readiness to cut off without any hope of return, or these people, mostly women (90 percent), would choose another way out.

Victims of False Memories

About fifteen thousand family members in the United States: fathers, mothers, grandparents, and siblings, have been accused of sexual abuse, and the number is growing fast. One-third of the parents who have contacted the False Memory Syndrome Foundation (FMSF, which tracks such statistics) have said that their children wanted nothing more to do with them, but they did not know exactly what they had done to cause that to happen. Some had not been told at all. Some had been accused of outright sexual abuse directly, and some had only heard about it through the grapevine, yet in every case their children (mostly women in their thirties) had cut off from them completely. Either the retrieved memories of the "survivors," as they call themselves, are true or their parents' impassioned denials are true, but it is impossible for anyone outside any given family to say cate-gorically, "This claim is true; that one is false."

We do know that about 300 survivors have now retracted their assertions. Let us assume, however, that of 15,000 current members of the FMSF only 1500 family members are telling the truth when they say they have never molested their daughters. Let us say that 150 are telling the truth, or even only 15. The ques-tion that still begs for an answer is why 315 young women would be so destructive and self-destructive as to invent such a story. Why would each young woman drive a car off a cliff with the whole family piled in with her? How did family relations become so full of hate?

Freud Fever

The infamous outpouring of retrieved memories began in the 1970s. At that time, clinical interests, a concern about child abuse, and the growing women's movement all converged. Minorities, usually silent, clamored to be heard, and there was an especially bitter backlash against the crime of incest, which had either been hidden away or rationalized for centuries. It has always been known that millions of children and young girls were the victims of sexual assault from their own fathers and brothers, but it was not admitted to the consciousness of most nations—an example of what Christopher Bollas called the "unthought known" in human history. This true crime coincided with the spirit of the times, namely that of victimization, and false incest, as well as true incest, became a magnet for all those who felt vulnerable in some way. In this receptive social climate, true survivors were less ashamed to speak up and ask for help. For those with an unnamed malaise who could not find the source, false incest provided it.

True incest survivors *do* suffer for years in mind and body, and so some women who suffered psychological trauma became convinced that they probably were incest survivors. As terrible as it is, false incest provided a single, strong, and focused explanation for years of wordless unhappiness for thousands of women. The retrieved-memory movement that had named the horror and brought it out in the open seemed to be such women's champion. After a while it produced a horror of its own: fathers were named falsely, and families were destroyed.

The Child Abuse and Protective Act of 1974 seemed to be another corrective to the Dark Ages; it was a federal law for the protection of children that promised immunity to anyone reporting child abuse. To make up for years of underreporting, even the most outlandish charges against parents or child care workers now had to be taken seriously by professionals, or they risked being prosecuted themselves. Many cases of true sexual abuse were brought to light by this act, but as there was an incentive to produce evidence or be found negligent, a self-serving bureaucracy flourished as well. Mark Pendergrast states, "The more cases they find, the more funds they receive, and the more vital their jobs appear," and so this good law also encouraged false accusations, including the rash of day-care scandals of the 1980s, which in the end cost the taxpayers and defendants millions of dollars, yielded jail sentences from contaminated evidence, and destroyed lives.

In some cases investigators badgered children involved until they got the responses they were after. "I'll let you eat. I'll get you a Popsicle, but only after you tell me [what I want to hear]. I know you know. Don't tell me you don't know. I know you know." If any child abuse actually occurred, it often was obscured by strong-arm tactics and unofficial posses. Any malicious rumor would bring out a retinue of righteous social workers and police and would raise an angry mob. Some parents turned into vigilantes, too, for if one child in day care was induced to believe that he had been molested, no parent could afford to doubt it, or to sleep easy thereafter until the criminals were punished. For example, as Frederick Crews points out, the McMartin nursery-school case in California cost $15 million before the case collapsed of its own absurdities.

The Courage to Heal, by Ellen Bass and Laura Davis, drew an immediate response, for it raised women's consciousness about the prevalence of incest. According to the ideas it expressed: bulimia or insomnia or feelings of unexplained malaise might be residual symptoms of childhood sexual abuse. This book cast an even wider net than the therapists of the retrieved-memories movement had, since it said flatly that if you think you were abused, you probably were.

Men as Villains

As incest was declared a crime of fathers, the era of the 1980s also had a new villain: man. The formerly blameless parent of the Freudian family suddenly became visible and menacing. In the Freudian heyday, fathers were the ideal. Boys wanted to best their fathers, girls wanted to sleep with them, and women envied them their superior equipment. The refrigerator or castrating mother had been the target of the psychiatric establishment from the 1930s through the 1960s, and women who had passively assented to this labeling and were ashamed of it now, were part of the backlash.

Also in the 1980s, women heard the shocking statistics that as many as one in every four of them had been abused by her own family. They also heard that male oppression began most brutally at home, and this was the era, finally, when men would be held to account for that brutality. *Courage to Heal* was militant and instructive about it: face the fact that you were abused in the family, and search for memories that support your intuition.

People wonder whether those therapists who promoted the search for repressed memories of abuse were cynical and malevolent from the beginning. Probably not. That happened in the second wave, when memory hunting and hauling parents into court were like a holy mission for the therapists and lawyers who recognized false memories of incest as a bonanza. Those of the second wave started to advertise their services in the Yellow Pages. Following the success of child abuse prosecutions, the way was clear for more zealots and ideologues to ride the "incest" bandwagon.

Because the complaint was incest—and it was a widespread complaint—some of the therapists were idealistic about the cause, indignant for their clients, and abandoned a professional stance. They were no longer neutral observers or interpreters; they joined the client's fantasies and soon were leading her into a frenzy for discovery. It became a *folie à deux* (as we will see in the case of Christine, below), wherein each party was gratified and formed a closed loop of mutual admiration. At this writing it has been reported that as many as a quarter of the 255,000 therapists now practicing believe that repressed memories can be retrieved and that it will take years and years to get to the bottom of them. This constellation ensures therapists a steady income for years, as well as blind transference love from the women who come for help. The second wave of opportunists and "incest counselors" was quick to realize the possibilities.

This frenzy has many causes. The retrieved-memory movement has borrowed Freud's ideas at the same time that they disown his treatment of women. Therapists often use his concept of repression to validate reported cases of incest, and yet they hate Freud for his final, long-term position that sexual abuse was a young girl's fantasy and her wish. It is a schizophrenic amalgam that has led to tragic results.

Freud, in effect, added to the scandal of undiscovered incest during the period of his intellectual dominance by turning away from it. The analysts who followed him, blinded by their own transference to Freud, were more willing to interpret what they heard as "incest fantasies" rather than true incest. Also, the fantasies do not raise troublesome ethical questions. The American Psychoanalytic Association, which was founded in 1911, held its first panel on actual sexual abuse in 1985.

Incest is mean and intractable, but incest fantasies are a source of delicious speculation and self-knowledge, and so in focusing on incest fantasies the therapist also spares himself the unseemly, the gritty, and the insoluble. As a result, although the retrieved-memory movement relies on Freud's concepts of repression, denial, fantasy, dissociation, and the unconscious as the basis of belief, the movement takes its revenge on him as well. In his long career, Freud wavered between incest as event and incest as fantasy, finally deciding on fantasy. The retrieved-memory movement is the apostle of the event.

The Appeal of the Retrieved-Memory Movement

The appeal of the retrieved-memory movement is in its vigor in facing down the ordinary social forces of silence and denial. Incest really happens; its denial is the fantasy. Today the Freudian view of repression is that an unwelcome fantasy like wanting to have sexual relations with your father is repressed in the unconscious, but the *fantasy* really happened, not the event. The fantasy continually strives to break through the repression barrier and the psyche keeps trying to push it down. Dreams, for example, pass the instinctual barrier only through disguise.

What further confuses the debate between fantasy and event is that fantasies of incest are experienced by most family members but are not tolerated by the adult mind. Thus they have to be repressed. A little girl's first choice for marriage is her father, and a father cannot not notice a blossoming daughter. When people live close together, their early sexual thoughts are, inevitably, of each other. The one who has these fantasies in later life is filled with shame and guilt, yet these thoughts keep breaking through the repression barrier. For example, the worst obscenity in the English language is *motherfucker*, yet it is heard everywhere, and, important for this discussion, it is always projected onto the other. *The search for memories of abuse is like an endless obscenity that is projected upon the other.* If an incestuous act is said to have been committed upon a child, it relieves the boy or girl from the guilt of his or her own fantasies: "Oh, it wasn't a fantasy after all. It really did happen, but *he* did it to me." As everyone has these fantasies, some therapists have their own guilt or shame, and they pull for more and more guilt-relieving projections.

The important thing to remember throughout this discussion is that incest happens. It is real. Fantasies about incest are also real. Incest is so primary an offense that people deny various aspects of it, sometimes the fantasy of it, and sometimes the fact of it. Both are true.

Courage to Heal gave hope to thousands of women living guiltily with bad memories just because it came down squarely on the side of the event that they had experienced and had been forced to deny; it promised many thousands of others who had fantasies of incest that there was always someone to blame. The book addressed the problem of incest and false incest by accepting every woman's claim as true. In all three editions published so far, this book encourages women to find the fantasies that support the event, joining up with Freud, who many years ago provided instructions for those therapists who go after memories. One of the great attractions of being a victim is that the activity is located elsewhere: In his book *Sex and Fantasy*, Robert May states, "The victim is acted upon, not the actor." As a victim there is no sense of oneself as destructive or hateful. For any woman who cannot own her own aggression, the position of victim, for all its troubles, has a positive lure. The retrieved-memory movement was designed to serve victims. As there is a growing feeling in the country that unless one is a victim one will not be served, women flock to it. Further, a victim must be absolved without question. In their therapy groups, for example, shared victimization is the basis of group self-esteem and identity.

The retrieved-memory movement claims that millions of women have been programmed to forget what was done to them. Incest, they say, must have occurred, the right coaxing will produce the right memories, and fantasies will produce the *event*.

Cult Memories

In his book *Making Monsters*, Richard Ofshe, a social psychologist at the University of California, tells the story of Christine. This story is especially valuable as a blueprint on how to erase one family from the mind and substitute a new one for it.

According to this story, a month before she was diagnosed with a terminal disease of the bone marrow, Christine, aged twenty-six, first came to believe that she had been sexually abused by her father. The new memories, not the disease, remained the focus of her therapy and the center of her own interest in the last years of her life. In the end she believed that the sexual abuse had caused the fatal disease. Her father was an alcoholic who often lashed out at her mother and could not remember his own behavior afterward. Christine's mother, Helen, divorced her husband when Christine was eleven and tried to raise her two girls alone. When she was laid off from her job as a drafter, the family went on welfare for a while until Helen started a small business from home.

As grown women, Christine and her sister, Janice, lived in Colorado a few states away from their mother but often reminisced with her by phone about the good times they had had when their father was away. They remembered Christine's record as a straight-A student and her popularity in high school; her mother especially recalled Christine's likable high-school boyfriend.

After a year in therapy these easy reminiscences and good memories ended, as Christine's therapist began to suspect that her symptoms pointed to sexual abuse. Christine grew up to be a fussy eater, drank too much, and had few childhood memories. As her father was often out of control, it was easy to identify him as the perpetrator.

Christine joined a group of incest survivors and bought several books that confirmed her worst fears. *Courage to Heal*, especially, reminded her that "dysfunctional patterns often accompany sexual abuse" and that "victims often use alcohol as a way of forgetting." Through her individual therapy and her support group, she learned to relive old memories, and one day she had a physical flashback and saw her father's hands on her breasts and his penis in her mouth.

Later, Christine began to "remember" with the aid of her therapist that her mother was also an abuser since she must have known about the abuse. Though Christine's mother wrote and tried to call her. Christine and her therapist weighed her mother's phone call about Christine's illness and decided that it was abusive and manipulative. They wrote her warning her not to call again. In the future, Helen might write to Christine only if the letter contained the right kind of apology, like, "Christine, your childhood was hell, and I didn't help you," or "Christine, you are entitled to be angry about it for the rest of your life if you wish to," or "Yes, Christine, I saw you being abused, and I didn't help you."

Helen was frantic. Her daughter was dying, yet she and her therapist were determined to make Helen jump through hoops rather than deal with the current awful fact of Christine's life. As Christine's sickness worsened, her vision of her childhood grew bleaker, and she found solace in telling the story of her abuse. She gave speeches around Denver, telling the community what it felt like to be a survivor of sexual abuse who had a terminal disease. She later came to feel that being a survivor had caused her disease. Her parents had a lot to answer for.

After another few months, Helen got a letter from Christine's therapist telling her that Christine might allow a visit if Helen (1) read *Courage to Heal* and (2) went into therapy. Helen did both in order to see her daughter, but when she was finally allowed to see Christine, she was weak and emaciated. The therapist read Christine's list of complaints. Among them:

"When I heard you say, 'Both my girls are smart and talented,' I heard you saying that alone I didn't possess any qualities worth noting." And, "When you said that you loved all of your children equally but let Janice enter a beauty pageant but I couldn't have short-term modeling school."

The list of accusations never got beyond this banal level of complaint, while Christine's mother sat there and watched her daughter die. Reading the long list aloud, the listener is riveted by this incantatory list because a daughter is dying, because of the solemnity of the proceedings, and because a "victim" is sacred and does not notice at first that all the items taken together are the complaints of a sulky child. None of them warrants depriving a mother of her dying daughter.

Christine concluded by saying, "I believe the scar tissue in my bone marrow is simply a manifestation of my belief that I was rotten to the core and [of] my wish to please you by ceasing to exist." This charge is not silly, of course, but damning and unanswerable.

Helen could say only, "I'm sorry, Christine. I'm sorry, baby. I'm so sorry for everything."

At the end of the meeting, Christine's therapist handed Helen a list of the accusations to keep. Christine died a few months later, leaving instructions that no one in her family be notified of her death until a week after the memorial service.

The Charm of the Cult

This is a cautionary tale of induction into a cult with no telltale signs. In effect, a woman enters into a cult with society's blessing because this cult declares that it is devoted to eradicating incest. Incest is repellent. Of course it is. Who would dispute it? Yet what if it is a false claim of incest? The word incest itself, like Holocaust, with or without emphasis, is enough to close down most minds, yet we know that Holocaust has often been used frivolously to make political points.

As in a cult, the door is barred to the old family, and the new one becomes the repository of all hope. The cult's principles become the inductee's way of life. How does it happen? Robert Jay Lifton, a psychiatrist who is an expert on cults, explains it this way:

> An emptied self merges with a charismatic figure who provides a direction in life and a single-minded message that excludes the old family and a ready-made identity outside of the family. The cult provides a flight from confusion. The milieu is controlled from without—it is usually remote and without transportation—and inner communication is controlled by intense group process. Fasting, chanting, limited sleep, lectures and encounters keep the emotional intensity high.

In Christine's case, each new memory added a black mark against the family. The grievances mount until they are insurmountable. All who are not for this new version of family history are *against* the survivor. (Like Christine's sister, Janice, for example, who was not invited to her sister's memorial service.)

Helen was given some hope that she would be able to gain admission to her daughter if she recanted, was purified, and performed some of the rituals of the cult. She was required to read the manifesto of the cult, *Courage to Heal*, thoroughly, go into therapy, and could not phone Christine even to ask about her daughter's illness. When she learned how to ask to be forgiven in the right way (that is, learned the right mantra), she could write to her daughter. Her actions had to be monitored, however (in Helen's case by her daughter's therapist and her own. In conventional therapies, this is a violation of privacy).

The therapist has now confidently moved into the role of God-like parent. As Christine was dying, the therapist allowed Helen to visit, but only after imposing more conditions. The mother was kept at arm's length while the therapist, in whose house the event took place, held Christine's hand and prompted her long list of charges.

There used to be a court of inquisition in England called the Star Chamber, which sat without a jury. This court, which was abolished in 1641, became known for its arbitrary methods and severe punishments. In this Star Chamber, Christine was the prosecutor, her mother was the defendant, her therapist was judge and jury, and her sister was banished.

Christine's transformation was now complete: All good memories of the old family had been systematically obliterated and replaced with bad ones. Christine was no longer someone's daughter; her family had been reduced to jargon: perpetrators, enablers, or victims.

Survivors bond together into a group and find new strength in the group. "Even though it was traumatic for me to realize that everyone in my family abused me, there was something reassuring about it," one woman reported in *Courage to Heal*. "My life suddenly made sense." The path to this closeness is through similar memories, and life as a survivor becomes a way of life, a social cause, and an obligation. "We must always assume and tell them so, that they have held something back," Freud said about eliciting memories. In this steamy atmosphere, every survivor is at the center of interest, and each new tale captures the surrogate family's attention in a way that was never possible in the familiar old way. The elaboration of horrors at each meeting takes each survivor deeper into the group family and provides a common memory bank for everyone. The group also provides the unconditional love of infancy. The therapist is gratified by her own loving action; everyone in the group is gratified by unlimited approval. Since no one is frustrated, the therapy itself becomes an endless infancy.

We all struggle to tell ourselves the true and real and single story of our lives, but we usually fall short because our story has too many straggling ends. The "incest" story is unified and vivid; there is nothing gray about it, nothing ambiguous, nothing uncertain, nothing unfinished. All the added details—like satanic rituals and cannibalized babies—round out a single story.

A cult promises a new realm. These very special experiences go beyond the human to the supernatural, and for that reason they promise *immortality*. If you are subject to terrible satanic abuse, it may be that in a past life you were a terrible person. But a *past life*, however bad, gives the hope of redemption in a future life for both therapist and patient.

RETRIEVED MEMORY
AND CUTTING OFF

Although it is true that there are therapists in the retrieved-memory movement who plant allegations in the minds of patients, we must be careful in assigning blame. In this victim-ridden age, in no sense is the patient just another victim. For the allegations to take root, the patient must be suggestible to begin with; she must have a psychological readiness to be convinced. Pendergrast cites the case of a retractor, Leslie Hannegan, who decided on her own that her father must have molested her. When one therapist disbelieved her, she went shopping until she found one who did. Hannegan subsequently recanted on her own; she had some ability to observe herself, some residual sense of subjectivity.

In Christine's case, her psychological readiness to be a victim was exploited by her therapist. To quote Lifton, "An emptied self merges with a charismatic figure who provides a direction in life," and it is for this reason that cult members seem robotic: they have given over their selves to someone else, but *they* have sought out the God-like person.

Having given herself over to her therapist, Christine had

no wants or desires of her own, and she could not imagine that anyone else had feelings of their own either. Thus, she treated her mother—the other person—as an impersonal object. For Christine, her mother, Helen, had become like a child's swing or a car, incapable of feeling but quite capable of causing harm if the swing breaks or the car rolls down a hill.

Both of Mark Pendergrast's daughters cut off from him, accusing him of unspecified sexual abuse. Early in her separation, his younger daughter made the chilling comment that her accusation was "nothing personal" and "in an odd way I have come to realize that she was telling the truth," he says. There was nothing personal in it, because in her eyes neither she nor her father had any subjective life. Pendergrast is thus coerced into playing a part and is locked into it. *This is his daughter's internal drama, yet he cannot get out of it.* His daughter can accuse him of sexual abuse or not accuse him of sexual abuse; it is all equal to her.

The Container and the Contained

In the Pendergrast case, the father *contains* his daughter's projection, and that is all he can do in relation to her. He tries to climb out of this container by begging his daughter to reconsider, by learning everything there is to learn about the false-memory syndrome, and by writing a book about it. For her part, she has projected part of herself into him, and he cannot escape the projection. She cannot hear his pleas for understanding, because her subjective self is gone. Yet he is stuck with his all-too-subjective feelings of anguish and devastation because he cannot reach his daughter.

Paul McHugh, a psychiatrist, reports this same bland indifference in another young woman. When her mother proved to her that her uncle could not have abused her, as he was overseas during the time cited, her daughter was momentarily taken aback. Then she said, "I see, Mother. Yes. Well, let me think. If your dates are right, I suppose it must have been Dad." And with that, she began to claim that she had been a victim of her father's abusive attentions and nothing could dissuade her.

Christine was cruel to her mother, yes, but if she had been told that she was cruel she would not have known what the word meant, because she no longer knew what it was to be kind or cruel. The situation was: "I have no feelings, therefore you have no feelings." She did not distinguish between her mother and a chair or a table; she did not make that distinction about herself, either.

In Christine's view, *she* was the prisoner; *she* was oppressed. She contained her mother's thoughts and could not escape them; *she* felt like their slave. That was why she monitored each word from Helen until she found a hidden message, and that is why Christine tried to stuff her own words back into Helen: to change the message. As a way of regaining control, Christine tried to make Helen use the words and designations (*abuser* and *manipulator*) that she, Christine, gave her. Making Helen feel safe was a full-time job, however, and Helen never seemed less dangerous to Christine, no matter how much she was monitored or chastised. Christine could not fight this enemy; she was convinced that Helen was stronger and would try to take her over.

Cutoffs spread within a family, corporation, or sect because it always comes down to an issue of us and them: Who will join the strong and wrong one? Who will stay with me? I am weak, but I am right. With false accusations of incest, a father or brother is the first target, but later the accusations spread to other family members, until the mother and most of the siblings are also named. The others, brothers or sisters, must be cut off too if they refuse the survivor's designated story because if the survivor were to accept their reality, she would feel like their slave. If she cannot control the other person's "stronger reality," as Helmut Stierlin termed it, she must either cut off or submit to it.

The Sibling Domino Effect

Pendergrast reports on the *sibling domino effect*. For example, one daughter of several retrieves incest memories and tells her sisters about them. One sister accepts the survivor's reality, proves it by joining the first sister, and this alliance strengthens their resolve when together they hold their parents' feet to the fire. It develops that if incest is not a common bond, they still have many other old scores to settle. Perhaps the psychological readiness of the first sister empowers the others; perhaps it just provides the right climate for them to display their own omnipotence. In any case, some of the other sisters then develop their own memories.

In the sexualized climate of the 1990s the area of offense has broadened to include date rape, sexual harassment, emotional incest, and "lookism" (sensitivity to the violation of personal space). One daughter accused her father of "incestuous behavior" when he told her his worries about his job! A cloying sexuality is in the very air.

The Absolute Need to Cut Off Comes First

Even in a situation where a father respects boundaries and stays well within them, these days his affection for his daughter may still be called emotional incest. There is not much point in drawing up guidelines for what constitutes "emotional incest" either—as some college campuses have done for date rape, for example—nor will it help for fathers to be more aloof with their daughters, because the sexualized climate is hospitable to any sexual accusation. Even so, the absolute need to cut off comes before the first accusation is made.

The wonder and mystery of it is the urgency of the need to

cut off, as in the young woman who decided that if her uncle could not have been her abuser, that it must have been her father. When there is an absolute need to cut off, parents old or young, strict or permissive, cold or loving, religious or irreligious, or well organized or chaotic, are all dismissed. There seems to be no one pattern or family type affected.

A NEED FOR TOTAL CONTROL

A clue to the riddle of the overriding need to cut off lies in the way individual "survivors" process family interactions. For example, the twenty-two-year-old who says that her father is being incestuous when he tells her about his job has already converted him to an invading object. In her mind, she has no way to protect herself against him. Without an "I," she has no words to tell him that, although he may not know it, he sometimes seems intimidating or invasive. In her mind, the word invasive is the same as an act of invasion. She must either control him or be controlled by him. There is nothing in between.

Omnipotence Is Total Control

Omnipotence is total control. It was a sense of omnipotence that made Christine direct her mother to write to her only when she had learned the right words to say. It was a sense of omnipotence that made her try to teach her mother the right words before meeting with her, telling her to say: "Christine, your childhood was hell, and I didn't help you," or "Christine, you are entitled to be angry." To feel strong, Christine had to redirect the aggression she felt coming from her mother and control its impact. When Helen apologized and read *Courage to Heal*, as directed, and then agreed to see a therapist, Christine discovered yet another excuse to complain that her mother had not fulfilled the terms of their "contract" to the letter. No matter what Helen did, the case against her was already closed. There were two reasons for this: (1) the cutoff occurred before it was rationalized by a "reason." (That may have been why Mark Pendergrast's daughter told him that there was "nothing personal" about her cutting off. She spoke the truth; it just had to be.) And (2), omnipotence is the only way to gain total control; anything else leaves one vulnerable. If Christine were to have negotiated with Helen, for example, it would have meant submitting to her persecution, and Helen would thereby have "won." If Helen were to have won, Christine would have been overwhelmed with either envy or hatred for her mother, and that, too, would have given Helen the power to control Christine's feelings. As long as she had anything at all to do with Helen, Christine would have felt like a victim. The only way to get away from a dangerous person with so much power is to treat her as though she has been annihilated. That is the omnipotent way.

The Essential Ingredient

Without a psychological readiness to triumph in this way, however, no woman could be coaxed by a therapist or group or cult to go this route. Omnipotence is its own reward and needs no other. Why is that?

An abused child learns to take care of herself, and that becomes her pride: feeling that she can prepare for any crisis on her own. From an early age such children strain to get away from being held since care is an intrusion and a threat. Even if mothering improves, it is hard for these children to give over or let their guard down. This is the experience, for example, of an abused child who is removed to good foster care. He will fight being well treated because he has learned that he is safer alone.

Since he does not know when he will have to be on his own again, he will keep his guard up and his skills at self-preservation honed.

The Accidents of Life

What feels like abuse is not always deliberate abuse, but only a bad period in an ordinary loving family. It can occur when adults are too distracted themselves to take care of their children. Fathers lose their jobs, and the family has to move. A beloved aunt dies. Mothers get sick or depressed and worry over money, or have to work long hours to earn enough money to make ends meet, or have too many children, or are too young and foolish to attend to the never-ending job of child rearing. A child may be in distress from bouts of colic or in pain from surgery and cannot distinguish whether the pain comes from inside or out. His mother may be gone for serious or trivial reasons, but an infant cannot tell the difference. It all feels like pain and abandonment to him.

There are also everyday unattunements between a mother and child owing to temperament. Perhaps his lusty assertion is treated as aggression, or his exuberance is baffling to her quiet nature. A mother may be grieving or ill for a time and emotionally unavailable, and the child may associate his mother with pain. One patient told child psychoanalyst Jack Novick, "Unhappiness is the smell of home."

In Winnicott's famous phrase, most mothering is "good enough." The English pediatrician and psychoanalyst believed that the inevitable lapses in good-enough mothering equalize over the long haul of child development, and children learn to soothe themselves in gratifying ways when their mothers are gone.

For a sturdy and trusting child, then, part of the pleasure in herself comes from being connected to her mother. Yet when the feeling of having been on her own continues too long, when she has been sick in the hospital as an infant, farmed out to a woman whose rhythm is different from her mother's, or the child herself is just temperamentally and genetically inclined to turn inward rather than out, the child learns to provide for herself.

Novick believes that children who feel abused or have been abused manipulate the direction and the impact of aggression because taking charge keeps the misery under their own control.

If the child hurts himself—by head banging, let us say—he controls the pain and the direction it comes from before his mother can hurt him by ignoring him, hitting him, or treating him coldly. When pleasure is out of the question, pain is always available and is a way to feel something. He becomes attached to his pain because he is in charge of it, can be sure of it, and he is now attached to his mother *through* the pain. He now has a psychological readiness for the omnipotent solution because he has withdrawn from the real relationship. He has learned to use himself for gratification more readily than he can use his parents. In fact, after a while the pleasure in everyday competence—such as his parents demand in schoolwork, for example—is a threat to the omnipotent system because it leaves him feeling ordinary. Defeating his parents is a greater triumph.

There are remnants of these old childhood feelings in all adults, even in those who are empathic. There are times when everyone has a nameless resentment toward another, when the loving connections vanish and the other seems less than human. When things go wrong, the adult feels like an abandoned child again, and this nameless resentment takes over. For example, Lillian wanted only a modest wedding, but her mother worked as a housekeeper and did not have enough savings to pay for it. Lillian knew the circumstances well and had, in fact, worked her own way through college. Still, she felt so outraged about her mother's not paying for the wedding that she stopped speaking to her for several months. A long time later Lillian reported, "I just went crazy. I felt so *abused* by her, although I knew how much money she *didn't* have!" She was mature and hard-working herself, but Lillian felt frustrated by her mother and slipped back into an abused mode as though she were a child.

To a small child, parents are either all good or all bad, depending on whether they give you what you want. When a small child who is trying to do things herself toddles away from her mother and is then hauled back, the child is furious with the mother. As an adult, during crisis, she may again project such angry feelings onto her mother that she is not able to remember anything good about her. These feelings recur throughout life.

Spencer and Eleanor, a married couple in their early forties, had three small children close in age. Eleanor, a lawyer, was the principal wage earner; Spencer was a sculptor. Eleanor arranged for in-house child care with a back-up sitter as well, but during one busy month she had to fly to Atlanta several times. Spencer, who was in the middle of his own project, was resentful that he was the second alternate for child care and was called upon to help during Eleanor's absence.

His resentment toward Eleanor did not pass. He lived with her in two modes. In one he thought of her as a steamroller who knocked him flat; he had no control over her. She went to work and abandoned him with the (other) children and had no regard for his feelings. In his other mode, he noticed the dark circles under her eyes; he realized that she was overworked and not getting enough sleep because one or another of the children awoke during the night. Although he observed these things about her and told his brother about them, he could not bring himself to help Eleanor, because he felt so abused.

ALLOWING PARENTS TO GROW UP

The hardest task of adolescence and early adulthood is to allow parents to be grown-ups who have human failings.

According to Tyson, it feels like a great injury when the idealized parents of infancy—that golden couple who knew everything—turn into the dull and diminished pair the child knows today. Everyone is a little paranoid at some time (the abused mode), but judgment, conscience, and empathy are also part of the human repertory. Most people eventually find room for the other person in their thoughts (the observing mode). Lillian had already realized that her mother would have paid for a wedding for her if she could have, and one night Spencer will get up to a crying child and let Eleanor sleep. He cannot sustain his hatred of her, because he is also susceptible to her loving qualities. Each in their own way, Lillian and Spencer, like all of us, are the retractors of everyday life.

ACTUAL INCEST VERSUS IMAGINED INCEST

When the father actually violates the child, the child can no longer look upon her father as protector or have playful fantasies and dreams, including sexual ones, about the father. The actual event now defines their relation. They cannot get beyond it.

After "incest," which is a fantasy, the situation is the same. *It is as though incest has actually occurred* because the relation between father and daughter is defined by the accusation. The daughter has put into her father her wish and fear of his abuse, and the father will live in fear of her desire and her potential for damage. It may occur to him that she had an absolute need to cut off because she sensed his incestuous wishes and is punishing him for them. Between them, they have caused it. He now carries the essence of the trauma, and to the extent that she still carries ghostline figures within her, she does too. As they live under its shadow, it may feel to both of them that actual incest has occurred. With all its horror, the fantasy seems like reality.

PART II

Reconnection

10

BRIDGES
FROM
CUTOFFS

In his book *Victims of Memory: Incest Accusations and Shattered Lives*, Mark Pendergrast tells the story of Olivia, who had been in therapy for about a year when a friend interested her in a six-month training program for young people through a mission group. After extensive training, she volunteered to go to Central America, but even though she was out of the country, she still kept in touch with her counselor, Tricia, by telephone. Tricia had convinced Olivia that she, Olivia, had been abused by six men, including her father, grandfather, and brother. Fran, Olivia's group leader in Central America, bluntly disagreed. She doubted that Olivia had been sexually abused, and Fran did not hesitate to tell Olivia that she was always worse after her overseas telephone sessions with Tricia. Olivia was furious at Fran's words, but she did hear them.

When she came back to the United States, Olivia went away to college, but she still had faith in her retrieved memories, even though her friends at college were as skeptical as Fran had been and told her so. She looked for another therapist. On the advice of the new therapist, Olivia bought the *Courage to Heal* workbook and started searching for memories again.

That summer, however, Olivia had an experience as a camp counselor that finally shook her faith. "I was in a boat on the pond with a beautiful, sweet, sad little ten-year-old girl. She said, 'Counselor, my daddy is doing something bad to me when he sleeps with me in my bed.'" Olivia knew from that moment that she was not like this child. "She remembered. She always remembered," Olivia said of the child. Olivia had no such memories.

There are several elements in Olivia's story that helped to free her. First among them is that the foreignness of Central America was a constant reminder to her that there were different kinds of problems in the world and different ways to solve them. Next, she was still in touch with many friends from her old life who doubted her "memories." At college she met other nonbelievers. The seed of doubt that her group leader had planted in Central America was reinforced by this network of friends at a time when her connection with her first therapist was weakened owing to distance and time and a lack of reinforcement.

Even so, Olivia had tried to hang on. When she ran out of money for therapy she had tried to remember the therapist's ideas by following the *Courage* workbook. Yet, finally, the child at summer camp opened her eyes. The episode ended when she was deprogrammed in an imaginative but effective way, complete with a closing ritual, by a friend in her college dormitory who made her shout three or four times at the top of her voice, "I was not sexually abused." She wrote to her counselor and told her the same thing. Then, ceremoniously, she ripped up and burned her copy of *Courage to Heal*. It was a liberating moment.

Cult members are usually isolated geographically or in a compound, as they were in Jonestown or Waco, to keep the message pure and intense, but retrieved-memory cultists are scattered. Sometimes light from without filters in as they go about in the world. For example, another retractor, Shauna Fletcher, had read a newspaper article about a family who claimed that they were the victims of false memory syndrome. Shauna sought them out because she had known their daughter in group therapy and realized that they could not be satanists. Olivia, also, had too many outside resources to be a cult member, among them skeptical friends and enough of the "I-you" way of relating left within her to hear them.

Women in the retrieved-memory cult need skeptical friends and family who are not put off by being rebuffed. Such authority figures as a trusted minister, teacher, or doctor are used to risking the anger of someone who disagrees with them and can help or serve as guides. If outsiders take the risk and persist in questioning whether charges are true or false, perhaps they can plant the seed of reason.

The Airless Transference

Transference to a cult depends on *airlessness*, a merger with one strong figure or their like-minded followers. Where the beliefs are wrapped tight and continually reinforced, it is harder for the light to dawn. When one daughter's belief bolsters another's (the sibling domino effect), the bulwark against reality is stronger. For example, Mark Pendergrast's two daughters supported each other's resolve, and one of his daughters also lives with a woman who has cut off from her father. In effect, this threesome—daughter, lover, and sister—forms a new family. Any one of these women runs the risk of being ousted from her new group if she moves to rejoin her old family. Thus, if she recants, the stakes are higher.

Pendergrast also writes about a father who lost three daughters to false-memory syndrome and another who lost four of his five daughters. These new family groups of daughters, like cults, are formed against the old family, and they define themselves by their opposition. In the ordinary course of things, separating adults marry and form new families, which become part of a larger family network. The bond is there, called upon without words; the associations are unthinking and voluntary. When children sever the generational line, they are fighting something essential in their connections; they are going against the grain.

Separating

Tyson states that the goal for new adults is to come and go as grown-ups, establish friendly relations with their parents, and feel independent of them at the same time. To be independent of her parents, each young adult must also allow her parents to be separate from her, which is hard because she is saying goodbye to safety and to the parents who will always be there. The hardest task of adolescence and young adulthood is to give up the golden, larger-than-life parents of infancy because it seems that without them there is no protection. Yet if she continues to see them as an idealized couple who can never fall from grace, she will be bitterly disappointed in them as she changes herself.

When an adult child in her thirties or forties complains that her parents are not what she thought they were, it means that she still sees them as she did when she was a child. She is deeply hurt that they have turned away from her, a child in need. If she sees her parents with a child's eyes, she will expect them to treat her like a child.

No one's development is linear or perfect. One can feel like a passive and helpless child at any age. When life gets too hard, a married woman with children of her own may retreat to the old feeling that her parents have abandoned her. An absolute need to cut off comes from a feeling of having suffered irrevocable damage at the hands of one's parents. The parents are abandoning the child by sending her into the world before she is ready; they are punishing her, as she sees it, for an old offense such as having sexual feelings for her father. The complaint of "incest" makes use of these feelings but turns them on their head: the parents are too close; the child is passive and victimized.

This process is clearest in young people who are leaving home for the first time. Those who are fearful of setting out by themselves for a life on their own may find it impossible to comply. Olivia, for example, described herself as someone who was pampered and adored as a child. Growing up was paradise. As though to linger at home, she became clinically depressed as a senior in high school and stayed in bed for weeks. She was having trouble separating from her family, which is not unusual at eighteen. Her therapist, however, invented a more elaborate diagnosis. In therapy, Olivia retrieved memories of abuse by six men, including three family members. The men in her family became ogres in her mind, and that forced her to leave. In effect, she scared herself out of the house. When she went to work with the youth group she had not yet accused her family but was distancing herself from them; she was trying it out by living far away.

Within a year she was successful at several tasks in the outside world: the mission group, college, and as a camp counselor. In two of them (the mission group and camp counseling) she was in the parental position herself. In that year she was confronted by two stark experiences of sexual abuse: she was nearly raped while in the mission group, and as a counselor, she heard the terrible true story of a ten-year-old. She learned the difference between fantasy and fact from her own experience.

The Ghostline Personality

When a daughter or son claims incest when no incest has occurred, they are signaling that something has gone seriously wrong in the separation process. Development has derailed. She or he has failed to use the actual world of persons and things and has instead turned inward. According to Bollas, this special inner area is bound by a "ghostline." When an actual person crosses the inner line, the person who has her own reality "deliberately alters it and defines it as a unique inner presence." In other words, she invents the person as she needs him to be; she invents his presence, his person.

The two young women mentioned earlier who so baffled their listeners did exactly that. They did not respond to actual people; they were on automatic pilot. Remember that Pendergrast's daughter told him that her accusation of incest was "nothing personal"; that is, reality was whatever she had made of it. McHugh's patient was satisfied that if her uncle was overseas and could not have raped her, her father must have done it. The real person is irrelevant "except as a sponsor of its transformed double." Those beyond the ghostline are changed into ghosts of themselves so that the subject can control them. The ghostline world is sheltered and cannot be permeated by reality. Thus, if a formerly loved member is not allowed in, "It is nothing personal." That is just the way it is. The real person disappears into the imaginary world.

When the Light Dawns, How Much Do They See?

I think my son has gotten stuck on a limb and is now uncomfortable to be there, but not sure how to get off. A part of me thinks he needs to face what he did and why he did it and change his view of his past and me. Another part wants to help him, let him slide back into contact and relating. I wonder about what another layer of "let's pretend" will do.

—A mom

There is an item in *The FMSF Newsletter* about a couple nearing retirement whose lives had been "a living hell" for several years owing to the "recovered" memory of their thirty-three-year-old daughter. They were afraid that she would insist on a court battle and take all their savings. Their daughter, who had never lost contact with her siblings, wrote them to ask if she could come home, but asked them not to speak of the past. They agreed. "For two years this continued. Last week, she retracted fully. She wants to apologize to her father, but he isn't ready to accept it."

Actual retraction takes time because these sons and daughters are emerging slowly from an alternative world, an inner world of their own making, to the world of a living family. They do not know how to make the transition. It is not clear how they managed to take that first step out of the inner world, but somehow they must take the next one and flesh out the ghosts within them. From reports in the newsletter of the False Memory Syndrome Foundation, each returnee seems to have a slightly different plan. One of them wishes to act as though nothing has happened; another will explain herself by letter and hopes there will be no discussion. A third exonerates one parent but not the other; two years later she recants entirely.

Relating

Masud Khan, an English psychoanalyst, has written about how to relate to someone who is distant and mechanistic but who would nonetheless like to make contact. To do so, he distinguishes between relating and a relationship.

> *Relating* is limited to each encounter and its continuity accrues cumulatively from such encounters over time; whereas, at least for me, a *relationship* can start immediately and there is no vigilant anticipatory caution about how it will develop into mutuality. *Relating* has less mutuality but more *intent rapport* [joining]

at the time. It is also "framed more consciously, at least by me, in terms of my personal responses and reactions. . . . In relating, each retains a separateness and distance, which allows more room for playing."

Moving Carefully Across the Psychic Distance

Long-term "separateness and distance" should be acknowledged, as Khan suggests, by moving slowly. On the one hand, it would be like denying the experience of everyone concerned to ignore the past entirely, and, on the other hand, it is too ambitious to try to deal with the pain of the lost years all at once.

As a protection for both sides, psychic distance will not, and should not, vanish overnight. The returnee must expect a slow transition to the world of relationships. She will move toward her parents and away again. After all, for some reason that she cannot quite remember, she fled from them. As well, her accused parents cannot be expected to feel safe with her all at once. She left for mysterious reasons that have not been explained, and she may do it again.

Their own feelings toward her are complicated. They love her because of old connections, and they hate her for the damage she has done. The barrier will come down slowly, with much testing on both sides. Khan speaks of "dosing"—short visits with serious talks—meant to introduce real contact, but gently. The people involved are both strangers and intimates. Powerful issues lie just beneath the surface of every meeting. The final resolution, "a relationship," is far down the road. The first step toward it begins at the periphery of common interest, at the periphery of the family. The way the family speaks with the returnee is "framed more consciously" than in a secure relationship because there is a definite agenda. The agenda is a reconnection. After that comes expiation, catharsis, and reconciliation. To move toward these goals during early, middle, and later visits, there are several effective strategies.

The Problem with Family Therapy

These are complicated long-term issues that call for a protected setting with a family therapist who will "frame [them] more consciously," to recall Khan's term. The therapist's primary task is to help the family redefine themselves without the false incest label, because both the trauma and the label have paralyzed them. Although a good therapist will be able to deal with the feelings of hurt and outrage in an even-handed way and see the family through the trauma, there is a special problem when dealing with families in which there has been a false accusation of incest.

The family has already been victimized by therapists, and it would be understandable if they never wanted to see another one. Perhaps they can work out some of these issues with clergy, a doctor, or a mediator.

In any case, the family needs to know the issues that have to be worked through so that they can move past the trauma of a false accusation of incest. Even if the family members choose to work on the problem themselves or take it to another professional, they should try to answer important questions for themselves because their goal is to learn to talk about them on their own. The questions that are raised are ones that come up in most psychotherapies.

The family that discusses these difficult matters on their own must keep their goal in mind, which is resolution of the cutoff, and develop strategies that work toward it. Every meeting introduces the question of how close or how far to come to one another; every meeting introduces the question of how to deal with unspoken issues. It is these two issues: the bitter past and closeness or distance from one another now that call for strategies of resolution. The family cannot pretend that they are reuniting under ordinary circumstances, nor can they flood each meeting with feeling. The movement must be slow; reconnection is a process.

Reconnection Takes Time

Although both of the examples that follow fill in a family history, the second one moves a little closer.

1. "Uncle Harry sold his house and lives in Florida now. Would you like to see it? The new owners added a nice deck that you can see from the street."

"Aunt Louise has three grandchildren. The little girl, Amy, is about four, and I think she looks just like you."

Closer to the issues: months later, after several "relating" visits:

2. "I'm sorry now that I missed grandma's funeral."

"I'm sorry, too, She had a special feeling for you, the first born." (Expressions of remorse should come from the returnee first because they reflect a change in psychic distance. They should always be heard and mirrored.)

"I can take you to the cemetery, but if you want to go alone, I'll make a map." (This intervention allows the returnee to regulate the distance.)

"Speaking of being sorry, I'm sorry that I missed Ricky's growing up. When you come next time, please bring some early photos."

Family Issues Reflected in the Cutoff

1. "You know, Linda, the idea of 'child abuse' may have come from me. I used it against your dad in the divorce."

"Sexual abuse. Here we go again!"

"No kind of abuse. I was desperate and reckless."

2. "You know, Mom, I was talking to Hattie [her cousin], and she reminded me that her mother ran away from the family and how hard Dad took it."

"That's true. She was gone eight years, and it really broke him up. I'm surprised Hattie told you that."

"I knew that all my life, and I noticed how it got to him. I think I wanted to get to him too."

"Why was that?"

"When I was in the hospital all those times with ear troubles, he never once came to see me."

"I don't like the man, but give him his due. He was working on the Alaska pipeline for almost two years. You cut off from me, too, remember, and I practically lived in the hospital!"

"Maybe, but the way I remember it, you let them keep me there and torture me!"

Changes have occurred in the family since the returnee was last a part of it, and the first example shows how to reenter at the periphery of the family's recent experience. The second example comes a little closer to serious family events during the cutoff: the death of a grandparent. Even so, the mother keeps her distance, which is a good rule, for months and perhaps for years. After all, none of them will forget that the old distance felt so wrong to the returnee that she had to cut off to get it right.

In the third example, there have been many visits and time between them to absorb their emotional impact, and the mother and daughter talk more freely. They look at the family system—past cutoffs in their family history—and touch on the daughter's terrible accusations. The mother uses a discovery she made about herself, that she had accused her ex-husband of child abuse, and "relates" it to Linda's same accusation against her father years later. Linda had discovered before her own cutoff that her father's sister had cut off from the family. The daughter has also observed on her own that she had an old resentment against her father and was paying him back for it. As mother and daughter set the record straight, the daughter finds that her old resentment is based on a distortion.

Both mother and daughter relate affective incidents to each other, and so the accusation is no longer a one-way street. There is both "relating" (the dosing affect) and the beginning of a "relationship" in that vignette, that is, they talk back and forth, turning things over in their minds together. Reinventing the family relationship has the unexpected benefit of clearing up some old distortions in the family history, and when the relationship is further along, some good memories from the good old days will return. There is no cookie-cutter, how-to method for such grave reconnections, but the issues involved are always the same: allow for a gentle reentry through short visits. Start at the periphery of family affairs; the serious issue should be raised in "doses" at each meeting. It is useful to think of reconnection as an extended process with an early, middle, and late period that will keep changing its contours, as old parts of the old relationship are reworked. The limits of the new relationship will become clearer further down the line, especially between father and daughter, as shown later in this chapter (see the section "Working Through").

How to Relate

Cutting off, like any other plague, must be demystified to be conquered. We have learned to do this with illness: first with tuberculosis and cancer and AIDS, and then with death itself. That means talking about it. Unfortunately (or fortunately), there is no lack of examples of cutoffs in everyday life, as well as natural and man-made disasters that result in cutoffs. These disasters can serve as bridges to personal discussion.

Some American fathers who cut off from their Vietnamese children have reunited with them. A neighbor cuts off from a homosexual son and then claims him when the son contracts AIDS. There are the parents who would not go to a wedding because the bride was of a religion different from theirs. Yet, in the aftermath, reconciliation often occurs when the couple has children. There are parents who honor their lost children, as, for example, in the case of the "disappeared" young men and women in Argentina who were abducted fifteen years ago by their government and are presumed dead. But they have not been forgotten by their relatives. Their mothers, in white head scarves, demonstrate every Thursday in a major square in Buenos Aires. There is the fugitive student who was wanted for manslaughter in Boston. Her parents and brothers and sisters had not heard from her for twenty-three years before she surrendered, but they celebrated her birthday every year nonetheless.

Making Bridges

An absolute need to cut off is the issue. It is an issue that cannot be avoided, because the traumatized parents will not be able to suppress their anxiety over the idea that they may lose their daughter again. In an early visit, someone in the family must ask the others to start thinking about how they can talk about what happened. "Start thinking about . . ." is a way to be serious without being confrontational. It helps to repeat the phrase at subsequent meetings, without pressing beyond it.

Asking permission to talk about the cutoff is serious but nonconfrontational in itself and sets the tone for the whole process. Once others begin to contribute to the discussion, the feelings about the years lost because of the cutoff should be allowed expression. A time limit for each meeting is reassuring, for serious talk is unfamiliar and emotionally draining. A fifteen- or twenty-minute discussion is long enough, as long as everyone agrees and contributes to it and the feelings expressed are genuine.

What has happened is tragic, and there is no way to gild that. Talking about the cutoff is unpleasant, yet talking about it is the first step in repairing it, and that is the incentive. Talking is better than walking. Everyone has had the wish to leave the family and its obligations. Perhaps the nonleavers in the family will recognize this in themselves and admit it. What makes one person leave and another stay? someone may ask. The only good that will come from this long and painful cutoff is a new way to talk in the family, which aims at preventing any repetition of the trauma. Yet if that is the outcome, it would be a fine and a powerful one.

Working Through

There are many issues to work through, time after time, before the family can be a family again. Many families have been to court to rebut charges of abuse; some have been under house arrest; and several fathers have been put in jail and are still there. The families involved are deeply hurt and deeply angry. Eventually, however, unless he is dead, the accused father and the accuser will begin to speak. One woman suffering from false-memory syndrome passed out notices to the mourners at her father's funeral that her father had raped her. The scenario that follows illustrates a confrontation after a false accusation and a cutoff. Confrontation, even if more muted than the one described below, is a necessary part of working through.

A father and daughter meet seven months after the daughter made initial contact after cutting off. They both know that she is back to stay. She can risk raising old issues. He is still very angry.

"Well, Debbie. You, here? Where did your mother go?"

"To the vegetable stand. She'll be right back."

"Then I'll get in the car and catch up with her."

"Wait a minute, Dad. I'll go outside with you. I want to tell you something my therapist told me."

"Don't 'therapist' me, Debbie. You're forty years old. You've given us grief we'll never get over, and you haven't learned a thing."

"I think it's all right if we stand in front of the house waiting for mom."

"What do you mean, it's all right? Oh, I get it. You're right. I wouldn't be alone in the house with you for all the tea in China, and your mother has already told you, I hope, that we don't ever want you to sleep over."

"I know you can't forgive me, but at least we're talking . . ."

"Come off of it! Every time I see you I want to take the strap to you, old as you are."

"I don't blame you. It's not that kind of therapist, you know. This one says I was acting out old resentments and never got over my rage that Kevin was your favorite."

"Oh really. Then maybe this one is not the usual nut job, but that doesn't excuse your doing what you did. But he's wrong about one thing. I liked all my kids the same."

Debbie, in the example, is starting to figure out why she was so alienated. A worrisome trend so far among many other retractors has been to blame the retrieved-memory therapists for what happened, but they will not learn much about themselves by shifting blame.

The family might risk going to a therapist if family members inquire carefully before making a choice and then screen the therapist before committing themselves. Here are some questions to keep in mind: First, the family should ask the therapists they interview what their views are about the retrieved-memory movement. Has the therapist ever treated anyone with newly found memories of incest? Has the therapist treated any survivors of true incest, and how do they know the difference? This is a necessary question because of the family's experience, of course, but also because of the number of therapists who have believed in retrieved memories at one time or another and who still may believe in them.

Is everyone really the victim of someone else? Were these "survivors" only empty vessels? If Debbie can "own" the damage and figure out some way to make reparation to her parents—concretely or symbolically—she will be taking charge of her life, and she will find her voice by using it to question herself. Why did she have to destroy herself and her family in order to leave them? Will this need to hurt herself and others play itself out again under other circumstances? As the family meets, they will be looking for answers to these questions.

Debbie's father told her that he cannot get over the fear of another accusation of abuse from her. He has told her point-blank that the trust between them is gone. When a woman accuses her father of sexual abuse when there was none, dream, fantasy, wish, and fear are treated as though they had been actual events. The woman who brings the charges believes them, and the father and family members suffer as though incest had occurred. Moreover, it may be a martyrdom without resolution because once the father has been accused, the family may never recover its good reputation. This is a difficult case to work through.

11

HEALING THE SPLIT

Open Adoption

One way to cut down on the splitting, fantasy, myth making, and alienation in the adoption process is to demystify it, making it real by involving both the birthmother and the adoptive mother. Open adoption does that. It addresses many of the difficulties previously discussed, including the importance of the birthmother, the mixed allegiance of the adopted child, and the ambiguous role of the adoptive mother. It answers the question of roots and identity.

During the 1960s and 1970s, in an era of increasing freedom from old social restraints, unmarried women were less ashamed about sex and more open about their pregnancies. They were also less compliant about turning over their babies to the authorities. On their own, they chose single motherhood or abortion. As a result, there was a decline in the number of infants available for adoption in the 1970s that reached crisis proportions in the 1980s. At the same time, there was an increase in infertility in the baby boom generation. Faced with long waiting periods, adopting families were willing to give up agency protection and confidentiality; birth mothers had more bargaining power and wanted to choose the people who would be raising their children and stay in touch with them.

As more birthmothers emerged from the shadows, it became clear that they were women who loved their children, gave them up with regret, and never forgot them. Simultaneously, it became better known, especially through the work on separation and attachment of English psychiatrist John Bowlby, that children as well as adults feel grief when they experience loss, even if the loss has a beneficial outcome. There was no way to have a "clean break," as adoption agencies that advocated closed adoptions had long believed possible. Open adoption is a way to reduce grief and loss: birthparents do not have to lose touch with their children to ensure they have good parents; the children need not forget their birthparents.

In open adoption, of course, the birthmother is known and real. According to Baran and Panoor, "the adoptee who is able to see, touch, and feel the birthparent can believe the fact that that person does care, but could not, at the time of the child's birth, take care of him or her." Open adoption also reduces the adoptive mother's negative fantasies about the birthmother. Because the birthmother had provided much information, one adoptive mother was able to speak to her child about his birthmother with genuine feeling, "I loved her before you were born."

In an ideal open adoption, the birthmother meets and chooses the adoptive mother before the adoption takes place. The birthmother remains in the picture to provide family history and memories. As time goes on, the adoptive mother shares the child's upbringing with her through photographs and visits, and the child meets his mother and his genetic family. Even if she wishes to disaffiliate later, the birthmother helps in the transition at least and, ideally, leaves knowing that her child is in good hands.

Open adoptions usually begin with formal agreements and are kept alive by relations between the two families that grow less formal over time. While every relationship is different, the first year is the time of the most intense contact between the two families, and, understandably, the first month of the new arrangement is the most stressful. Adoptive parents want to be alone with their baby, while birthmothers seem to need contact. Once they have signed the final papers, however, there is a reversal, and the adoptive parents are ready for more contact with the birthmother, with whom they have a special rapport. The third or fourth year after placement, the birthmother and the adoptive parents typically recommit to the relationship, though less intensely than during the first year. Sometimes the birthfather also becomes involved at this time. The best relationships seem to grow slowly and steadily as years pass, gradually including more of the extended birth and adoptive families until the adopted child has a strong support network. Because open adoptions are new, their fate through adolescence and beyond is unclear.

Open adoption is not a panacea: The external contact it provides must translate into a sense of secure and unified parenting within the child, a psychic solidity. We do not know yet how that may happen. We do know that the more splits there are in a child's life, the more pernicious the effect. Therefore any attempt to heal the split, as through open adoption, is a move toward synthesis. Although it is too early to tell, it seems that when the birthmother is in the child's life as an "aunt" or good friend, sharing vital information with him, it has a benign effect. Also, these days more birthparents than ever involve parents and grandparents of their own, which provides a stabilizing network for the child.

Since the 1980s couples who want to be parents have blanketed small-town newspapers throughout the United States with advertisements that solicit contact with birthmothers. There is a new kind of openness. Transracial adoptions are always "open" about what they are because the difference in race of parents and child is obvious. Birthmothers today do not hesitate to ask agencies to help them make the right match for their child. With an agency's help, a birthmother in California placed her child for open adoption with a mixed-racial couple (the father was Japanese). She felt that the match was exactly right because the birthfather was also Japanese and the adoptive mother had once given up a child for adoption herself. With a more cordial climate toward minority issues in the United States, birthmothers like this one have become more assertive about participating in their child's life after adoption occurs.

Although some adoption agencies have been enlisted to participate in this plan, they are constrained by confidentiality. Many states still seal most adoption records and do not encourage open adoption. The legal barriers in closed adoptions protect the privacy of all three members of the triad, but they also deepen the splits between them and complicate relations later. In closed adoptions, for example, the adoptee coming of age is usually eager to search for his birthmother, and the adoptive parents can be brought to see that it is in their own best interest for the adoptee to search. Yet, on the side of the birthparents, who can say how many are pleased to have an eighteen-year-old turn up on their doorstep?

Where there has been an earlier connection, through an open adoption, it is easier for the birthmother or adopted child to renew it even if it has lapsed. (For this reason, some birthparents and adoptive parents exchange social security numbers.) If the birthmother remains nearby, the nature of the loss is different, but it will not be easy for her to watch her child grow up in another family. Many of the gains in adoption, however, are long term and delayed. In time, when the birthmother knows that the child flourishes, her sacrifice may be redeemed.

The Psychological Benefits of Open Adoption

The best argument for open adoption, and a profoundly motivating one, is that the strength of the child's connection to his adoptive family depends on how he has come to terms with his birthfamily. The tie to the birthmother comes first because she gave him life, and it is this primary pull that makes the search for her in later life feel like a birthright. The child needs to conjure up his birthmother in his imagination in a way that seems right to him. Unless his connection to her has potential and can at least be a matter of speculation in his adoptive family, the secret fantasy about her becomes larger than life for him, and daydreaming about his birthparents intrudes on everyday reality. Like Lily in chapter five, he lives his life in two compartments, and the tie to his adoptive parents is weakened. In open adoption, the early and continuous awareness of the birthfamily makes the connection real. Contact reduces his feeling of isolation and his intense need to split and fantasize. Most important, from an early age he begins the task of coming to terms with his birthparent openly and with help.

Yet even if they could be convinced of the long-term benefits of an open adoption, the adoptive parents have many good reasons to avoid its complications. As new parents, they want only to establish a close relationship with their child. They would also like to put the child's past behind them and start fresh. Thus they will not be eager to embark on an uncharted course with the birthparent, a relationship that is sure to be complicated and highly charged. Such resistance is common to all adoptive parents and is self-protective. They must stay centered on the task at hand: learning to know a new baby and caring for him well. Involving anything or anyone outside that immediate context makes for extra work.

The adoptive mother must give herself over to the baby and cannot allow herself to be distracted. Is it not enough that she knows who must come first? Is it not enough that she feels deeply connected to the child? Is it not enough that she will attend to his every need at any hour? Is it not enough that she loves him as though he had come from her own body? Why does he need another mother? Besides, the birthmother might criticize him, interfere in his upbringing, or try to take the child away. If the birthmother is not present in one's life or consciousness, she cannot cause harm. Better to forget her.

The unconscious need *not* to be a *second* mother enforces this natural resistance. For the adoptive mother one way to defend against the painful thought that she is not the "real" mother is by coming to believe that she is the only one, that there is no other. She needs to believe this because the adoptive mother is as vulnerable as anyone else in the culture to the myth of the bad second mother and is, in fact, in that despised position herself. Because the new baby often enters the house without ceremony or transition, it adds to the uneasy feeling that something is not quite right. (Maybe she has stolen the baby!)

Claiming

Pregnancy is nature's way of making an active claim on parenthood before the baby arrives, and there is nothing furtive about it. It is evident for months, recognized with fond smiles from others along the way, and richly supported by tradition.

Adoptive parents have no sanctioned waiting period; they have to create one. They can prepare for the "birth" by putting themselves in a "pregnant" state of mind, taking better care of their bodies, losing weight, giving up smoking, slowing down at work, and taking classes in baby care—all in the service of creating a period of transition to another stage of life. Adoption agencies can help by having "graduation" ceremonies once the applications have been approved, as Lois Melina advises in *Adopted Child*.

Waiting parents must transform the child who is coming into exactly the right child for them. Early in this process of "parental claiming" they will also have to say goodbye to the ideal biological child they had envisioned. Now they must be transformed into the right parents for the child who is coming. It takes reflection, thought, and emotional investment over time to make this transformation. As a way of making themselves ready, some parents-to-be gather with friends to talk about parenting or to read a poem or story of their own.

Adoptive parents need to be authenticated. When other people think of them as parents and include them in this way, they gradually take on that role. Without time, ceremony, investment, and help from their friends, their claim might be shallow and perhaps fraudulent, the baby not quite theirs. There are other, more political, approaches. Thirty-five parents who took part in a parental claiming study took a strong stand against "the cultural prejudice and even biological hubris" that it was better to have a biological child than to adopt. (Here, on a psychological level, they were actively confronting the myth of the bad second parents, according to a *Journal of Contemporary Ethnography* article titled, "Somewhere out There."

What, indeed, is wrong with being the second parents if they are the ones committed to loving the child? Nothing, but it would be another mistake to think that adoptive and biological child rearing are exactly the same. In many ways adoptive parenting is different from, and more difficult than, biological parenting.

The Paradoxes of Adoption

The adoptive mother must bond with the child as if he were her own, yet she must be aware that he is not. Having transformed herself into her child's parent, it will be hard as the years pass for the adoptive mother to give up the illusion that she is the child's biological parent, since she loves the child as her own. The child is not biologically hers, yet is her own child. On examination, this seemingly hopeless paradox reflects the truth of the adoptive relationship. Further, it is linked to yet another one: the child will not accept the adoptive parent as his own until he has come to terms with the biological parent, because, as the psychoanalyst Edith Jacobson wrote, "the lost parent has become the most precious part of the self."

Once the adoptive mother recognizes that an important part of the child's self resides in his biological mother, she will want to help her child connect with her, if only metaphorically. Therefore another paradox of adoption is that, finally, it is in the best interest of the child for the adoptive mother to side with the birthmother. Until the nature of that first tie changes, there is no other course to take.

The Mother-and Child-Reunion

There are legends about the arduous quest for the abandoned child who has never been forgotten, and legends about the orphaned child who seeks through the world until he finds the good king and queen who are his parents. One adopted child in her thirties, Cheryl, roamed the earth, settling down briefly in one exotic country and then another, searching for her birthmother, waiting to find her so she could begin her real life. Cheryl and her birthmother, one or the other, birthmother or birthchild, must do the seeking: the two parts must be joined.

By the time she was thirty-three, Cheryl had lived for periods in Egypt, Italy, Japan, and Norway studying painting and weaving. These exotic countries somehow contained the mystery of her past, the mystery of her mother. She scoured their hidden villages looking, looking, looking—for what she did not know and could not say. Lackadaisical in everyday life, in these exotic countries, in these little villages, she was exacting. She covered the territory inch by inch; she canvassed the inhabitants from street to street and alley to alley. Although she traveled alone, she was never afraid. Instead she was somehow confident that she was leading a charmed life. As she knew nothing at all about her birthmother, she seemed to be acting out a fantasy about her own birth as it might have occurred in various places throughout the world with a benevolent mother watching over her. With so many fantastical elements, fantasy soon took over.

Cheryl's story is not too different from the generic story that leads to an unending journey. There is good luck and bad luck in the story. Some of the characters in it are rich and have a high position in the world, while some live in poverty. There is the drama of a special birth that affects the lives of everyone in the story. There is the bad luck of having been abandoned. There is the search for the good birthmother, and there is good luck for the searcher in being adopted by rich people. There is virtue and vice in the story: an ideal mother somewhere in the world, even while the child is at the mercy of the wicked mother who stole her. In this adoption story, the birthmother turns into the fairy godmother.

In Cheryl's story, she also kept moving out of a feeling of shame. She was fatherless and motherless, an orphan who was an adopted child. Her adoptive parents were make-believe parents, or "fake stand-ins" for the real thing. Her bitterness masked a sense of intolerable loss, which became clear to her in therapy and led her to begin a realistic search to find her mother.

Working Through Feelings

The birthmother, who may have a second family by the time her child sets out to look for her, may not wish to be found.

Even so, whether she wishes for a reunion or not, she never forgets the child she bore. There is, then, a magnet for her too.

One twenty-five-year-old woman received the final details about her birthmother's whereabouts late one Friday night. She immediately called her. "Was your maiden name Eloise Whitman?" she asked. The voice answered, "It was and always will be." The young woman continued, "Are you sitting down?" To which her birthmother replied, "How old are you?"

By recognizing the power of this connection, the adoptive parent not only accepts the inevitable, but she also makes a great gain herself. She actively aids her child in integrating his two mothers and minimizes the split between them. When they are both on the same side, who is the good mother and who is the bad one?

If, on the other hand, she does nothing about integrating the two parents, the child's sense of injury will not go away, and it may be inflamed. Usually it is directed to the only parents he knows. To him, it is as though his adoptive parents are deliberately keeping him from something important.

These challenges are latent issues in all adoptions. Open adoption simply guarantees that they will not be avoided: the child will ask about her birthmother; the child will want to know her background; and the adoptive parents will want to know when the child is really theirs. Open adoption is like an ounce of prevention versus a pound of cure, for these questions are the very ones that lend themselves to splitting and fantasy if left untended. For example, without a conscious connection to her child's birthfamily, it is easier for an adoptive mother to project her own negative feelings onto the birthmother. The child then becomes two different children to the adoptive parents: according to Paul Brinich, "our" good child and "their" bad child, which mirrors the child's splitting of his two sets of parents. If aggression is seen as the legacy of the biological parents and if the child is troublesome later in life, the acting out itself solves some biological mysteries insofar as it confirms a self-fulfilling prophecy. "Our" good child would never become the school bully, but "their" bad child might; "our" good child would not have learning disabilities, but "their" bad child might. In open adoption, the adoptive process is more readily demystified from day to day, and that demystification acts as a brake to splitting.

The three members of the triad have a basis for alliance in the experience of loss—a kind of loss that is particular to adoption. Birthparents and the adoptive child have lost the parent-child relationship; the adoptive parents have lost their chance for a biological child and immortality through that child. If both sets of parents can recognize what they have in common, that is another brake against splitting.

Both sets of parents go against the grain: one by giving their child to someone else to raise, the other by raising a child that is not theirs. One set of parents has suffered the loss of privacy through infertility, the other through blatant fertility. Both sets of parents fear that one loss will lead to more loss: the adoptive parents fear that the birthparents will be intrusive or abduct the child; the birthparents fear that being involved with the child will remind them of their loss.

Open adoption will not cure splitting entirely, but conscious awareness of its important themes will surely help all members of the triad. A great strength of psychoanalysis is that when the theme of loss comes up in the therapy of an adoptee, the analyst will listen for its various elaborations: losses big and small, what was lost, what was recovered, what the loss meant to the loser, and her dreams and fantasies about it. Taken together, these associations are what is important to that adoptee, and what is important to her is what will move her to act. Anything else is irrelevant.

These themes are examined again and again in different contexts to answer the question, "Whose child am I?" The biological family has to be invented, recalled, or otherwise brought to mind as part of the process. The successful psychoanalyses of adopted children is a reassuring reminder that the splits can be brought together. It is a lengthy and expensive process, but it is not the only method available.

Adoptive families can use the technique called working through, which is one of the main techniques of all dynamic psychotherapies, as a model for integration in their own homes. Working through means listening for a theme, hearing it out, hearing it repeated and elaborated in various contexts, and then weaving it together with other aspects of the adoptee's life. It also means encouraging these elaborations. Everyone, in the adoption triad or not, can have a richer, fuller life by recognizing the layers of meaning in everyday life.

For example, biological and adopted children have strong feelings about animals that are abandoned or come into the home as "adopted children." Just talking about the new puppy in the house and how everyone feels about her can be an important working through. On the other hand, failing to talk about an important issue when it presents itself in the family can bring on a storm, like the Matthews' old cat that was ailing and incontinent. One day, to their relief, she just disappeared, and the parents told their adopted six-year-old daughter that "a nice family had adopted Jezebel." That lie led to tears and a tantrum. The Matthews had gotten into this awkward position with the child because they avoided the issue, thinking that having the cat put to sleep would have been too hard on all of them.

Of course, the death of the cat would have been sad for everyone, but her abandonment to another family was perilously close to their daughter's own feelings about what might happen to her. Instead of joint mourning, the child's sense of having been betrayed by her adoptive parents as well as her birthmother became the issue. (The sudden disappearance of a member of any household threatens everyone in any family but may not have as much resonance as it did in this adoptive family, where the child had already lost her birthparents.) In everyday life, working through feelings, good or bad, seems to be the best way to heal a split, whether or not the adoption is an open one.

Eli

In the example which follows, the child's mother is scolding him for his slovenly ways:

"You didn't finish shoveling the walk, and you left the snow shovel by the back door, where anyone could trip over it! At fifteen you should know better."

"Aw, you're always on my case, like an old witch."

"What do you mean? I heard Dad speak to you about the same thing the other day. Is he a witch—or should I say 'warlock'—too?"

Eli spoke to the sky: "Sky, let me tell you about my adoptive parents. He's kind of nice, but she's a witch."

His mother, too, looked straight up at the sky and said, "Sky, ask him about his natural parents, why don't you?"

Eli's birthparents were alive, but he did not know them and knew nothing about them. Yet he had very definite ideas about them and even knew why he had these ideas. "They make me feel good when you don't," he answered.

"You've got them inside of you, is that it?"

"Yeah, I really know what they're like." Eli went on to tell her that his birthmother was beautiful, good, and very much like a movie star who played a sacrificing mother on television.

"You might have a point there," his mother said. "Where else did you get your good looks?"

"I'll bet you that she thinks about me as much as I think about her," he said defiantly, waiting for her reply.

"I bet she does, too. You grew in her for nine months. She wouldn't forget that."

Eli had not thought much about his birthmother until early adolescence, when his battles with his adoptive parents reminded him that he could have had another life, and then he began to speak about her all the time. This was painful for his adoptive parents, but they stuck to their policy of encouraging his expression. He thought that maybe, when he was married, his birthmother would come to live with him and help him raise his children. He was sure that she would have kept him if Eli's natural father had not run out on her.

Necessary to this fantasy is the feeling that Eli had one good parent in both sets of parents. One good biological parent, one bad one: an adoptive father who was all right and an adoptive mother who was a witch who stole him when his birthmother was out working to keep him. (Otherwise she would never have given him up.) He worked out this fantasy neatly so that it did not leave him too bereft, and he also seemed to be in some kind of dynamic transition: He split the parents he grew up with, split his natural parents, and retained a loyalty to his natural mother and adoptive father. His love for his adoptive father gives him something solid to hold on to, while his dream birthmother fulfills his fantasy. Most important, he is not cut off from his own struggle. He is engaged in it and seems to be on the way to realizing that his loving mother and his depriving mother are one and the same, the only mother he has ever known: his adoptive mother.

When Eli first rediscovered his birthparents as a way out of adolescent turmoil, they were both golden in his mind, and his adoptive parents could do nothing right, which is a classical good-and-bad split. Maintaining projective identifications like these (putting all the good or all the bad into one parent) takes emotional energy, and it is easy to see that the more a function (like the parenting function) is split in the mind, the more emotional energy it takes to maintain it. Everything else suffers. At fifteen, Eli was doing poorly in school, had turned away from his friends, and had stopped playing the piano. His behavior was a setback and a trial for him and the entire family. Yet with one good parent from each set, there were signs that he was on his way to integrating the two families. In Eli's adoptive family there had already been many years of easy discussion about the other family, and the pain they were feeling now was in the service of healing the split. In times of intense change, like adolescence, old wounds open, and old issues have to be worked through again.

In the past, adopted children had a higher level of pathology than natural-born children did because neither adoption agencies, mental health workers, nor adoptive parents were aware that the first order of business for the adopted child was to heal the split they had experienced. Eli's adoptive parents seemed to know. Also, Eli clearly trusted his "witch" mother enough to talk to her openly about his feelings. He understood that his birthparents were alive in him, that they were not "holes" inside him but active presences, and he was working out some way to include them in his life. Eli's adoption was not an open adoption, but, as his conversations with his mother show, his adoptive parents had always included his birthfamily as he was growing up.

Still, the weaving together of these two realities is easier with true open adoption. When the birthmother is available, she finds her own way to integrate herself into the family psyche. For example, one birthmother brought a single ornament each year for the Christmas tree of her child's adoptive family. Slowly and surely she made her presence known without overwhelming her son or his family or by offering him false hope. Her action serves as a metaphor for a careful and continuing process. This birthmother gave herself and the adoptive family a chance to absorb small changes. Taken together, these changes can heal a split.

In open adoption, the people involved are both real, with real qualities in evidence, and real with hidden feelings. What is missing at this point is a way to observe and comment on what is happening so that the healing can go forward. "Who are we to each other?" might be the question needed or "How does Tommy feel about my visiting so little [or so often]?" Others might be: "We [the adoptive family] need more time by ourselves now. Can we work it out?" "Is it too early to talk about Thanksgiving?" "Are you comfortable about the arrangement we made for her birthday last year, or should we do something else?" The families involved in open adoption usually have to chart a course for themselves and set boundaries without any guidelines. One birth-mother, who has been involved in an open adoption for ten years, says that it takes patience, tact, a willingness to make mistakes, get your feelings hurt, and try again. Although the process is sometimes difficult, even baffling, she says, "Mostly, we seem to find our way." The adoptive mother said that the birthmother made her feel "authentic." So far there have been rich rewards: a secure child in an extended family with two sets of grandparents, which means there is a feeling of inclusion for everyone.

The Adoption Story Revisited

In open adoption, the adoption story tells itself through meetings and memories. The story is ongoing and adapts to the circumstances of the people involved. When the adoptive parents do not know the birthparents, they will have to bring up the issue of his adoption extensively with the child. This is always a hard story to tell, even once, but in an open adoption there is a redeem-ing factor: the telling will redeem the pain of it. What was miss-ing from the old adoption story was the active involvement of both sets of parents to prevent or mend a split. Active involve-ment is part of the working through process. Working through means accepting the child's anger at having been given away and encouraging him to talk about it, draw it, or show how he feels about it. Who would willingly plow this frozen ground? Active involvement has not become easier, because there are too many harsh facts connected with the adoption story: the child was not wanted by his biological parents, and the adopted parents were unable to conceive a child of their own.

The hoped-for outcome is worth the effort: the child will have a more solid sense of himself and will be securely attached to his adoptive parents. These important rewards will help them in their resolve to tell the child her story fully. To tell the story fully, the adoptive mother must feel that she has come to terms with her infertility and grieved for the child she did not have, and that this very child whose story she is telling is the child she always wanted. What is new in the new adoption story is that the story itself must work toward weaving together the two parts of his life. Brodzinsky states, "In any adoptive family, the connection, or the severed connection with the past, must be surfaced, discussed, and dealt with. The telling and retelling of the adoption story begins the process of making connections."

The child will be angry and hurt whenever they tell her the adoption story, but if she is older, about seven, she is likely to be psychologically more resilient. Once she understands that she was given up, she is bound to have feelings of betrayal and estrangement. The parent must tell the adoption story in a way that allows for the child's expression of these feelings to develop. That is the other new feature of the adoption story: the child must be given a chance to work through her feelings as they come up.

Breaking the Mold

Now that we know that splitting is the single most harmful feature of adoption, the adoption story must be broken out of its old mold: both sets of parents must be alive in it. In the past, the adoptive mother raced through the story to the happy ending, haunted all the while by the shadow of the birthmother, the child's pain at having been given up, and her own pain in adding to it. No wonder she hurried through it! That story evoked feelings of being different and of loss and abandonment, questions about body image and identity, and feelings about the precarious coming together of adoptive mother and child. The child's response was not usually solicited, and he was left with his puzzlement and fantasies.

Even though the story is still painful, the adoptive mother will be motivated to tell it and to tell it often and in different ways if she comes to see that both she and her child will be stronger for it. This is not a one-time story or a bedtime story; it is his story, as it comes up day to day, in a friend's home or at school. Those are the times for the adoptive parent to tell the relevant part of the story again, soliciting the child's feelings about it in working it through. The aim, psychic solidity, is worth the effort.

Adoption themes come up in everyday life all the time and are not hard to recognize: Eddie, aged four, had been very interested in a neighbor's pregnancy, and Benita had allowed him to feel the baby as it moved. When Maria was born, Eddie saw the baby once and said he did not like it. Luis, an eight-year-old, daydreamed a lot in class. His teacher suggested he needed testing, but it occurred to his mother to ask him about his daydreams first. He was from Colombia, and the class was studying the rivers of South America. Adele, a beautiful six-year-old, began to have doubts about herself in first grade. She said to her father, "There must be something funny about me: nobody likes me; nobody wants me." Adele was a great favorite in her class, and what she said did not make sense. Her father knew that in her early school years the child no longer regarded her adoption in a positive light, because to be adopted, one must first be given up. The father and daughter talked it over:

"Sometimes adopted kids feel that nobody wants them when they realize that they started out in another family."

"You're not adopted. You don't know how it feels."

"That's true. How does it feel?"

"I'm not talking about that."

"It's true that I don't know how that feels, but I have sad feelings sometimes, and I hate it when things are not fair, just like you do. I felt sad when Grandpa got sick and nearly died. I feel better that he's still with us."

"That's two feelings. How can you have two feelings about the same person, Dad?"

"Sometimes feelings get all mixed up. I feel lucky and happy to have you, but I know you sometimes feel sad that you're not living in with your birthmother."

"I don't want to live with her. She didn't want me."

"She probably had two feelings, also. She wanted you but didn't know what to do about it. She was so young, she was sixteen, you know."

"When will I be sixteen, Dad?"

"Can you figure it out?"

She counted on her fingers. "That is young."

When the birthmother has always been part of the story, it adds another dimension to it. Like any good story, it leaves more room for the imagination. Adele had already speculated about where her birthmother might be living, whether she had other children, and if they looked like her. If she had a sister, she thought she would easily recognize her on the street.

Even minimal information, such as the state where the birth occurred, was something Adele could hold on to. She could look at maps, paint pictures, tell a story about her birthmother, or imagine what it might be like to live in the city where she was born. Adele had already been to Raleigh, North Carolina, where she was born, and her dad had stopped in at a state office to find out how Adele could begin her search for her birthmother when she was older. She and her adoptive brother and the parents who adopted them spoke about the other birthfamilies without embarrassment.

Judith Wallerstein, who wrote *Second Chances*, discovered that one of the reasons why the children of divorce have trouble functioning later in life is because there is an unconscious taboo at the time of the divorce: the grandparents never mentioned it, the clergy never visited, friends avoided the subject, and the children grew up feeling isolated and different. It is the same with adoption: returning to the story as it presents itself is necessary for both mourning and integration.

To help them remember, some adoptive parents return with their children to the villages of their birth in Colombia and Ecuador; American parents of Korean children have arranged for them to meet as a group and learn about the Korean culture. The ties to children like themselves, to their original culture, and to Korean teachers honor the past, make it real, and enhance self-esteem. It is a clear message to the child that the adoptive parents are on their side when they interest themselves in his life before adoption.

These parents have helped to develop a lore that is passed among newer adoptive parents: They have learned that adopted children have an inexhaustible interest in information about their background, even if it is slight, and so their parents have also learned to write everything down as it happens, rather than rely on memory later. They tuck away extra copies of all documents and photographs, which become "life books," in case they are lost or torn up in a fit of anger (oh, yes, that happens). Every scrap of information is precious. They also note and date any attempt to find out more information: how it came about, why it failed, who to contact at a later date, and so on. (Adele's father made a note of the name of the man he saw in the state office, dated it, and put it with Adele's papers.) They go over details often and help the child write letters to her birthparents, even if they cannot be delivered. They make adoption scrapbooks that show pictures of the places where the child was born and adopted. Sometimes they go to the faraway place of a child's origin. It is necessary, they feel, to offer to visit the agency or lawyer who arranged the adoption and to retrace steps, even if those steps lead to a dead-end, because it is more important to respond to the child's need to know than to display superior common sense. They have also learned when to stay out of it, too, by finding a support group for the child with other adoptees.

Rituals

Rituals enrich life. They add dimension to change and mark important transitions. As Thomas Moore said, they "nourish the soul." The thirteen-year-old who recites the blessing of the Torah for the first time or is a ring bearer at a wedding will remember and dream about that ceremony. Rituals place one deep within the experience as nothing else can.

Rituals are a most powerful type of working through because they repeat content, action, and form again and again. The coming-of-age ritual, especially as it is endorsed by the group, makes a child visible to the community in a new way and redefines her. This actually helps a child to grow up and helps her parents to realize that she has indeed matured.

Yet rituals are growing scarcer, perhaps because they heighten emotions and transcend the mundane, and no one has time for them. Religion, which sponsored them and contained their form, has been outpaced and abandoned by modern life, and with the absence of religion, for many people ritual has also vanished. Without the clergy, most people do not know how to create ceremonies for themselves and have not yet come to realize that they can invent new rituals themselves.

Adoption, for example, is almost devoid of ritual and suffers for it. Adoption is a time of great change and feeling and should be appropriately marked. The meaning of any ritual is to make people conscious of transition, yet, until recently, adoption has been a hushed and even secret act. The child became a member of the family, but with a shameful difference, and so there was nothing to celebrate, no wish for public record. The birth-mother was not encouraged to say goodbye; the adoptee never attended a memorial for her lost parents; and the adoptive parents were embarrassed to admit that they grieved for the biological children they did not have.

People in religious life have now begun to invent rituals for the painful events of everyday life that used to go unmarked. Sister Jane Marie Lamb directs a program in Belleville, Illinois for grieving parents that helps them with closure many years after the event. One birthmother planned a memorial service twenty-six years after she had placed her child for adoption. In the ceremony she lit a candle at the beginning of the service and blew it out at the end. She read aloud the story of Abraham's willingness to sacrifice Isaac and of Jesus' instructions that at his death John take Mary as his mother and that Mary take John as her son.

A farewell ritual for a child at the time she is being placed for adoption gives the birthmother and birthfather (if he wishes) a chance to say goodbye. Otherwise, in many cases, that adopted-out child lives on in her birthfamily as an unhappy cutoff.

Melina suggests that in open adoptions the birthparents' farewell and the adoptive parents' welcoming ceremonies be held together in the hospital chapel or in the birthmother's home. Holding the two ceremonies together would be unforgettable for both families and would provide the subject of an invaluable videotape for the adoptee later: he would see for himself that his birthparents had not rejected him in giving him up and that he was a full and equal member of his adoptive family. Such an entrustment ceremony is a profound way to come together from the beginning, but it is so deeply emotional that it probably needs someone from the clergy or a wise friend to officiate.

When a new child comes to its adoptive parents through a foreign adoption, for example, a welcoming ritual is in order: a naming ceremony, such as a christening, or a conversion ceremony. This ritual should be the first of many in an adoptive family. Welcoming a child from a foreign country begins as a courtesy and continues as ritual because so many elements are in place.

Here is an example: the Bryants adopted Tomas from Peru when he was seven. He missed his country and its food, and so his parents bought plantain and yams from Spanish markets, but they did not taste right to him. The family then got seeds from Tomas's region, planted a garden, and figured out with him how vegetables were prepared in his village. A few years later, as well as harvesting the produce, Tomas took over the cooking. Meanwhile, the family had also been learning Spanish at dinner. They began meals with a prayer, and after a while spoke only Spanish at the table. The Bryants realized that Tomas thrived when he had something concrete from his past to hold on to and show off, but growing the vegetables of his native village, eating them cooked in the traditional way, and speaking Tomas's native language helped the Bryants as well because it linked them with his birthfamily and country. Their world was enlarged. Together they evoked a dimension that nourished the soul.

Other parents focus on evoking the past through photographs and slide shows and then make an odyssey to the child's native country. The journey is ritualized by family planning meetings, the use of maps, and studying the geography and history of the people of the region. If they can, they make contact with someone in the village who might have known the child's family. When they arrive in these distant lands, they try to take their child to the very spot where he was born or found, saying a prayer, leaving a marker, or letting fly a balloon. When they can, they visit graves and hold a simple ceremony at the grave site. These journeys are a return to the important past to retrieve one's history and to find closure. The journeys restore place and people to the child who left them.

Lerner states that children who have lost a parent have an

almost palpable need for some real connection to the lost parent, as the psychoanalytic literature shows. It is not unusual for an adoptee to continue the search even after he learns that the birthparent has died: going to his father's old school or just walking around in his old neighborhood. The children also need something concrete to hold on to, like a ring or a letter. When there was nothing else available to one adoptee, he brought back some pebbles from his father's yard and kept them in a glass bowl. There must be some kind of commemoration.

Another way to remember is by celebrating anniversaries in a special way. Maya was born in Colombia on April 5 and arrived in Iowa City later that year, on November 9. Each date is honored by her birthparents with a special cake, one with an Andean peak on it, the other with a prairie schooner. Maya, now fifteen, is pleased. "I began life twice so I get to celebrate it twice," she says. Her adoptive parents, the Millers, help with the details and are there, standing by, but from year to year the celebrations are hers, part of the working through and integration of her adoptive self and birthself.

The adoptive process starts at the time of adoption, or earlier, and does not end until the child adopts her adoptive parents as her true parents. This finale is the result of integrative work and closes the circle. Choosing adoptive parents may occur after a search for the birthparent, and the emotional working through that a search inspires, or after psychoanalysis. It can occur, with or without the search, when the adoptive family has kept the concept of integration uppermost in the family consciousness while raising the child, for in some way they will have included the birthmother from the beginning, as was the case with Maya's adoptive parents. The Millers were part of her ritual and also stood by as onlookers while she worked out her feelings about her birthfamily. In some way the process itself can serve as a metaphor for the adoptive family's role: they create a friendly background for both families, but only Maya could have brought the two families together inside herself.

A successful adoption is a grand achievement and should be celebrated. It has been a long haul. The adoptive parent has to tolerate the frustration of not knowing the depth of the bond between herself and her child until fairly late in the child's development. The birthmother has to wait to learn whether her child is strong and capable in the world and whether she will forgive her. The adoptee has to deal with her hurt at not being part of her birthfamily, but, with luck, she comes to care for her birthmother, and she will be part of the ceremony.

The ritual might be a secular or religious one, but it need not be solemn. It could include songs and poems. The adoptee might give out prizes for patience and fortitude to everyone concerned over the many past years, including herself. After years of restraint, it is also a good time for an outpouring of emotion. There should be toasts and speeches of all kinds, funny and sad. Both mothers have felt judged; each has feared losing the child to the other. Now both are part of her, but she is also on her own. Above all, the ritual observance signifies a change in the adoptee's inner world: She has elected to be the child of these parents, a member of the family that adopted her, but she has not forgotten her birthparents.

12

THE BEGINNING OF RECONNECTION: ELLEN AND MEG REVISITED

"No, I would not give you false hope
On this strange and mournful day
But the mother and child reunion
is only a motion away."

—Paul Simon, "Mother and Child Reunion"

Ellen and Meg, the mother and daughter whose story is told in chapter two, eventually began to reconnect. But it was a long and difficult journey back. Meg's cutoff from her adoptive family lasted a long time because it solved problems for her involving both parents. After Meg cut off, Ellen tried to come into her life faintly, from a distance—through letters—hoping that Meg could tolerate this presence. Ellen hoped to come back into Meg's mind as a living human being, good as well as bad, and she believed that the single best thing she did all those years was to hang in, although figuring out strategies to reach her daughter took over her life.

The domestic details of everyday life parallel the slow and minute changes that occur in seeking to reconnect with someone who has cut off. There are few definitive moments in family life, yet the seemingly insignificant details of family politics show how a family is restructured over time. Ellen variously succeeded and failed to enter what Norman Rush called the "foyer of consciousness" of her daughter Through letters Ellen enticed, cajoled, preached, screamed, threatened, ignored, and sought to normalize the relationship.

Ellen wrote to Meg for five years, even though there was never a reply and no way to gauge the effect of writing. There was only a hope that the steady stream of letters would give Meg the message that her mother was there and waiting. Ellen thought of herself as "the stranger who begs": she had begged to visit, to take the children to various events, to have them spend some time with their grandparents, to come to their birthdays, to pick them up for short visits and deliver them back home. Meg contested all arrangements, but she seemed to be especially afraid of Ellen's being alone with either of the children. She finally agreed once, but she went along rather than let Ellen take a child to a matinee without her.

Ellen kept a journal to talk things over with herself. She watched for a change in Meg, but none came. She knew vaguely that she was waiting for some sign that she had entered the foyer of her consciousness: some small sign that Meg could hold her mother in mind for a minute or two as a presence that felt good, but there was little evidence of it. Whenever Ellen felt that she had caught her daughter's attention and dared to hope, Meg withdrew further.

Ellen felt that her strategies were all ineffective, even though she was by nature a "cheerleader": she continued to try to "relate" to Meg by bringing up the issues that were between them in fact or by metaphor, and sometimes she tried to interpret what they meant for Meg. She urged Meg to agree to family therapy sessions. Once she did, Meg insisted on choosing the therapist, who was a social worker who lived near her. Ellen and Ellen's husband, Will, went with Meg to the therapist for eighteen sessions, yet nothing changed.

The therapist never mentioned Meg's adoption and seemed baffled by her insouciance. Although family therapists are used to angry outbursts and division in families as being within the frame of things, Meg had left the frame, which stymied the therapist. There were no outbursts, and the division in the family was a severance that had taken hold. For her part, Ellen was equally stymied. Seeing Meg in the therapist's office, she could not yet comprehend that Meg had cut off permanently.

The core difficulty was that Meg had emotionally divorced from her parents, but they were not divorced from her. As her grandchildren grew, Ellen tried to establish memories with each of them, so that there would be a genuine connection some day. Through the therapist, Will and Ellen negotiated with Meg (like divorced parents) to visit their grandchildren, but Meg blandly evaded their agreements, and each visit was a new concession. She always came on time, perfectly groomed, silent, and indifferent.

Meg's posture in therapy was a counterpoint to the purpose of the sessions. Ellen had been hoping for an emergency that would shake up Meg's reserve and make her become real. One came. When Meg's father-in-law died, the burial was in his hometown a thousand miles away. Meg and Roger flew there with Jane, now four years old. Ellen and Will stayed with the new baby. When Meg and Roger returned home, Ellen and Will were packed and ready for the two-hour drive home. Meg was constrained, formal, and abrupt. She was humiliated at having asked her parents for this favor.

Because they were insistent, Meg exploited the power she had over them, however, and they spent seven years begging to be allowed into her life. If they had not asked, Meg would not have bothered to use her power. Meg was a bully only because her parents had forced the issue, and, because she was reserved, she avoided unpleasantness. She accepted their letters and took their phone calls. She came to family therapy, also, to avoid a scene. If her parents had simply given in to the cutoff, it would have been a relief to her. For she was a true cutoff: she did not know anymore who her parents were and did not notice that she did not know. She was protective when strangers—which included her mother—asked about her children.

The Long Road Back

Ellen's reconnection with Meg is a fair example of the long, hard road back for the victims of a cutoff. Nothing had seemed to happen for years at a time, despite her letters, her offers of gifts and visits, and her agreeable pose. There was rarely an answer, or the answer was no. When Ellen asked anxiously at the end of one family therapy session, for example, whether she and Will could visit her, Meg said, "We'll see" and forgot the request. Ellen felt that she had no choice but to push on. Otherwise she would lose her daughter and her two grandchildren. The children would lose their grandparents and also their uncle because Meg had also distanced herself from her brother.

Near the end of the fifth year of the cutoff, Ellen stopped pursuing Meg because Meg never responded to her phone calls or letters. She never initiated a visit. Out of fury, hatred, and despair, Ellen changed her tactic. She detached: she stopped calling, writing, and being heartily involved. She hoped to become an absence that felt uncomfortable. She hoped that the silence would resonate (felt presence, felt absence). The whole process was a journey in the dark, as there were no guidelines. In five years, she had sent forty-five letters into the void and wrote dozens of journal entries and trial letters. Trying to get her bearings, she sifted through what little came from Meg like someone panning for gold, but still she could not understand her daughter's action.

Trying to Reconnect

In trying to reconnect, Ellen's aim was to stretch that hoped-for second of recognition when it came to minutes and days and months. Yet trying to reconnect was harder than accepting the cutoff. As in negotiations for peace between warring countries, the position of the injured party is hard to relinquish. Ellen hung on to Meg, forcing a smile when she was with her and resenting her in private. She wrote Meg hate letters that she did not send and filled her journal with the details of Meg's latest outrage. She wished Meg dead because she had left her mother for dead without even noticing.

Many cutoffs start life over in new families. Meg was one of those. For example, an incest survivor may recruit her next younger sister into her private circle (the sibling domino effect; see chapter nine). In excluding the old family, they put down roots as a new group with an unshakable group ideal. They thus have a leader with a mission and a group born in opposition. When the group scapegoats an outsider, leader and follower are drawn closer together in the cause. This is the airless transference (see chapter ten) that occurs in the retrieved-memory movement, for example, or in a merged marriage (like Meg's).

Meg's Birthfamily

In therapy it became clear that Meg had a categorical need to make her own rules. She did not want to search for her birthfamily or have anything to do with her adoptive family. In becoming her own mother and having her own family, she had started life over; she was born again. She had no ties and no family tree.

Ellen thought that some change from outside would affect Meg and make Meg want her adoptive family in her life again. The most constructive change she could think of was for Meg to reconnect with her birthfamily. Toward the end of the family therapy sessions, the therapist understood that it would be helpful to everyone if Meg looked for her birthfamily. Meg finally agreed.

With the help of an adoptees' network that had grown expert in searching for lost birthparents, Meg learned that her birthmother was dead and that she had a living sister. She contacted Glenda, who was seven years older and lived in Texas. Glenda was enthusiastic about meeting Meg, and Ellen fell into the drama of their reunion as though it were her own. She pinned her hopes on Meg's relationship with her sister to help reconnect Meg to the world. With Meg's permission, she wrote an enthusiastic note to Glenda and gave it unsealed to Meg to send. Glenda replied with an equally enthusiastic note to Ellen, saying how happy Glenda was that her sister Meg had found her. Perhaps, Ellen hoped, Glenda would be the change from outside needed to bring all the branches of birth and adoptive families together.

Yet Meg was not able to sustain a realistic relationship with either her birthfamily or her adoptive family, because she had become her own mother as a way to solve the problem of her origins. An actual relationship with her birthfamily would have spoiled that illusion. Since her birthmother was dead, at least half of Meg's fantasy was reinforced. Having her birthsister and adoptive mother meet was too real and would have threatened Meg's fantasy of being her own mother. For Meg, her fantasy of having no ties was true, or was coming true.

THE RECIPROCAL CUTOFF

Family Politics: Double Binds and Collusions

As more time passed, Ellen cut off from Meg. Knowing that Meg had stored all her bad feelings in her, Ellen made a decision to keep those feelings no longer. Unless Meg was willing to take active steps against the powerful family system of cutting off that had been her legacy, she could not be immune to being cut off someday herself. Ellen made this decision without her husband, Will, because she felt that she was alone in it.

Because Meg's cutoff had been directed against Ellen, Will was in a difficult position. Meg had cut off from her mother entirely and moved a safe distance from her adoptive father, although she and Will kept in each other's orbit throughout. He did not want to lose Meg, nor she him, and he did not want to anger Ellen. If he openly joined either one, he risked losing the other. In family therapy, Meg's parents were treated as a unit, that is, as though Meg had broken off from both of them. The subliminal text—that Meg had cut off from her mother, leaving Will with split loyalties—did not come up in family therapy. Ellen tried to deny it in order to give her and Will leverage as a couple, and Will did not recognize the split. He thought of himself as the negotiator. Inadvertently, the therapist gave them each a way to handle this split, and the "solution" led to a collusion between the three family members.

Meg said that it would be all right if Will and Ellen phoned her occasionally, spoke to her only together, and did not talk too long. The therapist, however, thought that speaking to each other one-on-one would be a good way to reconnect. Ellen and Will started to phone Meg on Sundays according to the therapist's plan, each speaking to her separately. At the session following the first Sunday phone call, Meg reported that she could not stand the sound of Ellen's voice, so only Will continued to phone her.

The telephone calls from Will were mainly about making plans to see the children. Because of their need, and Meg's veto, these calls soon became the fulcrum for all family politics, involving power issues and double binding. (A double bind means that there are no real choices.)

How Collusion Works

Ellen, who thought that she was monitoring the collusion, became part of it herself since she used Will to reach their daughter. As the years went on, the collusion became untenable for Ellen: Meg kept making the conditions for seeing her and the children more difficult, as a way of demonstrating her power, testing Will's loyalty to her, and showing her contempt for her mother. In this way Ellen finally tried to cut off in reprisal, but it left her feeling even more defeated and guilty.

Meg once told the therapist, "I never invite them. If they want to come, he calls me." The less powerful member of a pair must adapt, Stierlin states, "to the stronger person's reality" as the price of entry. When Will called Meg, she established that she was in charge by refusing whatever he asked.

Sometimes by the second or third call she would agree to an arrangement, but sometimes she did not, because collusion is not about making plans; it is about showing strength. Above all it is a guarantee that two people will double bind the third, but in so doing, the alliance against the third person must be constantly tested or reinforced. In one of their family therapy sessions, Ellen realized how Meg and Will tested their alliance, and she wrote it down in order to remember the choreography, which was elaborate. Testing the alliance worked this way: Will told Meg in a family therapy session that both Ellen and he were sorry that she was unhappy when she was growing up and that he was sorry they failed to notice it. When Ellen was asked, she said that she agreed that she too felt that she had neglected Meg.

At this point Meg made her longest speech of the therapy, rebuking Will. "I don't know why all of a sudden you are a couple with her when you've been fighting for years. I'm afraid to speak to her because I can't tell when she's going to attack me, and that's what she does to you. What's wrong with you that you forget what she's like? I need to hear from you about your conflict-avoidance." Will did not answer, and the therapist asked, "What conflict-avoidance?"

Meg responded to the therapist, "Things were never good between me and her, but they got much worse after Jane was born. I didn't want to bring her into the city for a party she wanted to have for her." The therapist looked puzzled. Meanwhile, Will crossed his legs toward Meg, the shift in body posture being the affirmation she wanted. He then said, irritably, to Ellen, "I don't know why you insisted on that damn party!"

The telephone calls between Will and Meg had followed a pattern:

"How are you?"

"Okay, but Susan [or Jane] has a cold. How are you?"

"Okay. Say, we'd like to take Jane to the circus this month. There's one just a little north of you."

"Well, I don't know. That leaves Susan alone. I'll have to think about it."

"We could take her, too."

"No, she's too young."

"Maybe you're right, but you think about our taking Jane, okay?"

Here Will retreats. The double bind enforces her power over him. When he phones again, Meg may give him an answer, or she may evade it again, and he will not dispute it.

This is how Ellen, who thought of herself only as a victim of this collusion, became an active part of it, and how she came to cut off in self-disgust. Meg ruled on each request, and Will passed the ruling on to Ellen. Ellen petitioned her daughter for favors through her husband but did not speak to Meg directly because her wishes had no weight. Meg scrutinized each request to see her children that Will brought to her in the same humiliating way:

"Well, I don't know if Susan would really like going to the zoo," or, "The last time Jane went out with you, it took her a week to unwind." Ellen went along with it. Her need for her daughter and grandchildren kept her in the game.

Although they were not related by blood, Meg and her adoptive father were more alike than many genetic pairs: brilliant, competent, remote. They had an innate understanding of each other's hard-to-breach borders. Their wrangling seemed to satisfy their minimal need for contact, and it also seemed to be enough for Will to know that he could see the children any time he wanted. It seemed to have been enough for Meg to have said so. Neither one acted on it. The point Meg made with Will was that their alliance was the task, and she had given him her stamp of approval. Not only had she told him that he could always see the children, she had made him understand that he would always be her father.

"You don't feel that she is splitting us or that you are being disloyal?" Ellen asked Will somewhat tentatively, because it was as hard for her to believe that there was an alliance against her as it was for her to believe that Meg had really cut off. She was also deceived because Will was calm and kind and never angry at Meg, while she wanted to kill her. He felt that they were privileged to raise her and that should have been enough. That made Will more generous than Ellen in her own eyes because she wanted her daughter to be her daughter for the rest of her life.

Will's generosity extended to Meg's birthmother. He told Ellen that he regretted that Meg's birthmother did not want her as a baby and had since died. She would never know Meg as an accomplished adult. Adoptive fathers "are not hated in the same way as adoptive mothers," Will once explained to Ellen. To herself, Ellen had stubbornly denied the special affinity between him and Meg, but his words about the unbreakable tie between a father and his only daughter shook her. If she were to die tomorrow, she knew that the alliance between Will and Meg would continue without impediment.

THE RULE OF CUTOFF LIFE

The rule of cutoff life is that the one who cuts off must win. (Life is not fair.) The cutoff will act wronged to save his pride or defend behavior that cannot be defended. He must in no way be reminded of what he has done. During the period of family therapy sessions, Will called Meg to ask whether they could visit. She told him that they ("you people") could come if her mother would agree not to "talk about anything." Ellen reasoned that it would be a form of mindless masochism to continue trying to connect. She decided to refuse and told Meg, saying that she found the conditions humiliating.

At this point, after trying to connect for years, Ellen told Meg, "This way of being together doesn't work for me. I will write to you every year on your birthday and will see you any time you want to come and speak to me."

To Meg's husband, Roger, she said, "I wanted to tell this to you and Meg: the hardest thing for you will be to face up to your cruelty to me over the years—and for no reason."

He replied at once, "I hear you and understand you." Those were the first meaningful words he had ever said to her.

Movement, Movement, a Little Faster than a Tortoise

Three months later an invitation to Thanksgiving dinner came in the mail. The invitation was addressed to both "Mom and

Dad," and it had not been extorted from Meg over the telephone. She had sent it three weeks before the event, which meant that Meg had been thinking of her mother for a while; there had been no such sign before. On Thanksgiving, Meg was remote. Jane surprised her grandparents with a Christmas list; included in the list were the words "someone I can count on." Ellen recognized that phrase as her own. Jane had read a letter Ellen had written to Meg and remembered her words.

When Ellen sent Christmas presents, she took up the theme again and signed her note "someone you can count on." In reply came a note from Jane, thanking Ellen and Will. This was a breakthrough, but even more: there was a well of good feeling in it that came from Meg's family. Jane had also written, "I think of you a lot. When are we going to see each other again?" Ellen felt the words of the note might be a signal of change in Meg's family attitude or merely an independent voice. It was hard to tell.

Yet there were other, small signs of positive change from an unexpected quarter. When Will and Ellen said that they would like to visit over Christmas, Roger said that he would make lunch for them.

In addition, by then Ellen felt that her relationship with Jane would endure. As the children grew older, Ellen was sure she and they would develop stronger ties, and she reconciled herself to the loss of Meg. Ellen had grown weary of waiting for her daughter to change and she now pinned her hope on her grandchildren. This hope freed Ellen to visit Meg on a bright and pleasant winter morning and say, "I am sorry for whatever it is I did, and I hope we can talk about it."

Meg did not acknowledge the apology nor, indeed, anything at all. She said only that it did no good to talk about the past; the only thing that helped was to be pleasant to each other. Then she paused, having nothing more to say. Ellen tried to be pleasant.

If Meg failed to respond, neither did she show any alarm at her mother's all-encompassing expression of capitulation. Instead she confirmed, obliquely, that she could hold her mother in mind as someone who made a suggestion that pleased her. A few months earlier, Ellen had mentioned a book she liked, and Meg had gotten it from the library and enjoyed it. Did that mean that Meg was able to keep her in her mind neutrally or pleasantly for a time—a few days perhaps? Did that mean that Ellen had entered the foyer of Meg's consciousness?

The Beautiful and Melodious Sound of Ugh

Other small changes occurred about seven years into the cutoff. That spring Will sent Meg money for roller blades and told her that the children had asked about a skating party at the lake. She agreed that the children had been talking about going skating, which seemed to be her way of saying yes and marked a change in attitude. Another time, when Will suggested meeting Roger and Meg for dinner without the children, it was a simple offer from one family member to another, and Meg did not respond to the suggestion with a yes. She said "Ugh," which meant no, but it was a full-throated, human sound, the kind a teenager might make to a parent who had said, "I want to talk to you!" To Will and Ellen "Ugh" meant, "Maybe I'll be your daughter again, but don't think I'm going to talk about it." Even so, it gave Ellen and Will hope.

When later in the month they went to the lake for the weekend skating party, Meg and Roger were reserved, which was not unusual, but they barely spoke to each other. They were cool and civil, and there was an "edge" in their behavior. Ellen and Will skated with the children. In the evening, Meg and Roger disappeared without saying good night—perhaps a return to the bad old days when Meg treated her parents like strangers, or perhaps they had some trouble of their own. It was impossible to tell.

Ellen began to notice deliberate vacuums in the ordinary dialogue between them. There were no courteous requests: Would you mind? Is it all right with you if? Is it convenient for you? These lapses seemed to be elements of control by silent intimidation.

The next night, without seeming to speak about it between them, and certainly without speaking about it to Will and Ellen, Meg and Roger went to a movie, assuming that Ellen and Will would stay with the children. Their isolation had taken them away from the ordinary world and its ordinary courtesies. It was just too humiliating to ask, "May we?" for something. Using the words "please" and "thank you" would have meant that they had asked for and accepted a favor, which would have been intolerable for them. It was better when Meg and Ellen were alone. Tentatively, Meg would reach out. She would ask vague questions: about books or musicals, and Ellen would refrain from asking questions or overresponding. During the visit at the lake, Meg was more conversational, pursuing the details of a story avidly, as Ellen often did. In the process of reconnection, Ellen felt that Meg was "relearning" her, taking her in as mother in a way that pleased. Then, a week after their visit, Meg sought her out. She called one day when Ellen was improvising a recipe, and Meg volunteered to look it up right away in one of her cookbooks. More than that, Meg called when she knew that only Ellen would be home and invited her to a child's party. This was a major change from the grudging invitations delivered from Meg to Will to Ellen as a third party for so many years. It was much more than a change in manners; it was a change in feeling. "I'll have to ask Dad," Ellen said, "but I'm sure he will be delighted." Ellen began to believe that she had entered the foyer of Meg's consciousness at last.

Other things began to change, too. During the estrangement, Meg had had no curiosity about anyone in her past, including her brother. She never used the names of anyone from the past either, not of friends, families, or old teachers. Yet now Meg volunteered that she knew that her brother David loved living in the Northwest. Over the years, David had sent Meg photographs taken in the mountains; he had never been put off by her lack of response. Recently, without explanation, Meg had sent him photographs of the children and asked him about cameras. David told Ellen that Meg had not apologized for her absence but simply assumed that, when she was ready for him, he would come back into her life. And he did, because he had never left her. Indeed, like a neutral nation, he may have helped her to come back.

Less Global Cutoffs

Not all cutoffs are as global as Meg's was or as difficult to redeem. For example, feuds between grown children can many times be worked through when aging parents die if a brother or sister is willing to air the issues. One sibling is usually distrustful of the other over the care given to a dying parent, for example, and the resentment voiced about the matter often masks resentment over other family matters as well as old sibling rivalries. It is true that when a family reorganizes after the death of an important member, questions of power and rank are sometimes settled by the expulsion of another family member. Sometimes, after forty or fifty years of rancor and resentment, a family member will use the occasion of the death of a parent to expel him or herself, and this person cannot be retrieved.

On the whole, however, owing to the multiple connections between them, airless transferences are less likely between brothers and sisters and their spouses and children. There are, therefore, many ways to come together.

Divorce need not be a global cutoff, either. A man or

woman can almost always reconnect with his or her children over time. The noncustodial parent will develop other interests after a few years, and children in adolescence become disillusioned with the restricting parent they live with or disturbed by the implications of becoming the parent's "partner." They yearn to be rescued by the exciting outsider-parent.

A change from outside, then, can influence even absolute cutoffs one way or the other. Divorced men who have stopped seeing their children often start seeing them again when they remarry and have a home of their own; many adoptees rediscover their adoptive parents once they have made a good connection to their birthparents. Some victims of false retrieved-memories try to make amends and rejoin their families.

EPILOGUE

There are different paths to healing depending on the nature of the split and whether it is an individual or mass cutoff. For example, the adoptee must redeem his past in order to heal, and so must the homeless, the criminal, and the runaway, but the divorcing spouse must unlink from it.

Many kinds of healing are helped by a search for the past. Recently, Paul M. Lerner, a psychoanalyst in private practice, observed that those of his patients who had an early loss in childhood also had "a compelling need to seek out, rediscover, and then symbolically reclaim the lost object in the real world." It seems that in all cases of early loss, one must reconnect at the point of cutoff before moving on. Nor will the searcher find the lost person anew in the person of the therapist (a major belief of psychoanalytic psychotherapy); the quest takes one on an actual search to capture something directly related to the lost parent. One patient whose father had died when she was five could not put his death to rest until she had devoted herself to reclaiming him. She visited his grave site weekly; she contacted long-lost relatives, secured hospital records, and explored old photo albums. She was particularly affected by one photograph. In it, she was sitting on her father's lap reading a book, and he was looking at her with deep tenderness. With the help of this picture, she could recapture and fully experience the feeling, at age four, of having been totally loved by her father.

The adopted child, on the other hand, often starts out with only half its heritage—the adopted half—and often with the pretense that there is no other. The critical point made in the adoption chapters, the one that is essential to raising a healthy adopted child, is that biological parent and adopted child cannot be separated emotionally, because, to the child, the lost parent feels like part of itself. Although the adoptive parents are the psychological parents, the child will not fully accept them as such until he or she has *redeemed the life he or she never had*. This, of course, is true also of the runaway, psychotic, criminal or home-less person as well.

Another woman had a compelling need to take action in the real world and recover something concrete from an earlier generation. Her beloved grandmother's own daughter had died in an accident at age one, and the grandmother had treated her grandchild as though she were her daughter. This devotion made the patient feel that she had benefited from the death of her grandmother's infant daughter. She, too, felt compelled to learn more about the dead child and returned to their hometown to do so. Toward the end of her stay, she visited her grandmother's grave site and, realizing that she had not seen a stone for the infant, arranged for a marker to be placed next to the grandmoth-er's grave. After this incident, she believed that she had been able, finally, to bury her grandmother's daughter symbolically.

Both of Lerner's patients completed their mourning with a physical journey to reclaim a lost relative. As children they had not yet had the cognitive capacity to hold a lost loved one in mind or a concept of the reality of death. Their physical involvement, visiting the graveyard, searching out old photographs, buying a marker for the dead child, helped to evolve symbolic representations of their father and aunt. In effect, before they could symbolize the deaths, they had to go back, as though they were still children physically themselves, and deal with the deaths concretely through the artifacts surrounding the death. (Symbolization is a late stage of child development.)

It is also fascinating that the child who was so well loved by her grandmother as a replacement child had to return to their hometown to mourn the aunt she had never known. The grandmother's preference and closeness to this woman as a child made her feel her grandmother's loss of her daughter as a part of her (the granddaughter's) self! In this she was like an adoptive child who has experienced an early loss or the biological child whose father died when she was five: a part of herself continued to hurt. This is a good example of the unusual and unexpected effects of loss. This one could only be set to rest by the granddaughter when she returned home and mourned her grandmother's loss.

Divorce is a different kind of cutoff: it is a legislated cutoff. A successful divorce means unlinking from the marriage little by little, for the transition from married to single is made through distance and over time. In the chapters on divorce we notice that, when there are children, this process is often derailed. The reason is that the divorce, a cutting off, is at odds with the new drawing-in process that both parents must achieve with the children in the new circumstances. (Immigrants and stepchildren have this problem in an even more nuanced way: they must attach to the new country or family and leave the old one behind—but not altogether.)

After divorce, the noncustodial parent especially must invent a new way to be with his children to make up for the lack of a structured home life. In addition to all the many other disruptions of divorce, this dissonance in the two major processes—cutting off and drawing in—that characterize his life, goes on for months or years, and at some point many men just walk away from it. Recognition of this peculiar emotional burden is a great help in dealing with immigrants or stepparents as well as the children of divorce. It has to do with a balance between cutting off and drawing near. For example, studies show that the most involved father is the one who has joint custody, which indicates that these men have solved the problem of drawing closer to their children by establishing a home of their own.

But even when a man cannot solve this problem and ends by divorcing his children as well as his wife, the divorce need not be forever. A man can almost always reconnect with his children over time. Children in adolescence become disillusioned with the restricting parent they live with or disturbed by the implications of becoming this parent's "partner." They yearn to be rescued by the exciting outsider-father. The father of the adolescent boy, especially, can "rescue" him, just as he saved him from being overly close to his mother as a toddler when that need was outgrown.

When the children are angry and unforgiving as were Jerry's three children in chapter seven, a father who is eager to reconnect can borrow a leaf from Jerry's book. Jerry withstood the children's rebuffs and quietly persisted. He tried to engage each child separately and all the children together. The children would not come to him and so he went to them, repeatedly. He moved back into their community and became active in it. He explored their past life together by taking the children back to the old neighborhood. He offered them a richer life than he had when he lived with them by investing himself in them.

There is considerable hope that individual cutoffs like those that we have been talking about in this book will reconnect. But mass cutoffs like forced immigrants, the homeless, runaways, criminals and the psychotic, present special problems. Usually, these are extremely isolated persons who have lost the anchor of family. They drift mindlessly. Above all, the condition they find themselves in defines them to themselves and to others. When they can be reached, some of the techniques that are effective with individual cutoffs can be applied to them.

Unfortunately, remedies for reconnection of mass cutoffs will be needed on a grand scale over the next decade. This is because social systems, and sometimes whole countries, have and will fragment as the result of revolution, war, famine, and widespread disease.

Advancing technology, which makes connection easier, also makes it easier to disconnect. Huge populations are displaced, and displacement then has its own lures. Through global television, other places are made to seem more attractive. The airplane makes them easier to get to, and people will make almost any sacrifice in the hope of settling down in such paradises. With restless millions roaming the earth to find these Edens, stability and solidity in daily life are rare and precious anywhere.

In the United States as in other nations there are many signs of breakdown. The overloaded welfare system and the entire network of child protection agencies in the United States, for example, are on the verge of collapse. By the year 2000, one million children may be in the foster care system. Large numbers of these children are already showing the emotional consequences of being shuffled from foster family to foster family without ever really having had a place to call home. There is no break in the cycle of pathology. These children turn up in high percentages as homeless, as runaways, or at psychiatric hospitals and jails. Then, still cut off, they are out on the streets again.

On their own, the young and rootless of every nation lose touch with others and with themselves. Their isolation leads to a dangerous anomie and apathy: a deadening of feelings and indifference toward consequences. Fourteen-year-old children laugh as they are sentenced for murder. This new kind of cutoff, the death of feeling, is the one to fear most. The only solution for cut-off is connection, and these children of violence have none. Sometimes they do not even have one parent.

In the 1960s, there was some disaffection and play acting by middle class children in America who left their families and formed other ones to dance barefoot. Most of these returned home, safely. In the 1990s, there are makeshift surrogate families formed out of desperation, by those who have no homes to return to: gangs for the fourteen-year-old boy, babies for his fourteen-year-old girlfriend. This "solution" leads to more breakdown. Government grapples with the breakdown but cannot solve it with money or new programs. The only solution that has been proven to work is a one-to-one connection in small concerned communities, a solution which does not lend itself to legislation. There is some justification for the nostalgia for old-fashioned small-town life, for people miss the security of having a few sincere people doing their best in a neighborly way. Many people feel that the cutoff from the community—the loss of anything sustaining or nourishing—is one of the greatest losses of modern life.

Reconnection with someone who is detached from the community, such as the homeless person, the roving gang member, the parolee, or the alienated immigrant, always comes down to recognizing the individual's feeling of being different or out of place. Social programs fail when they neglect that element. The problem is how to convert what we know about individual psychology and apply it to greater numbers of people. For example, in the earlier chapters of this book we looked at cutting off from a variety of perspectives. We have seen how to recognize a cutoff-in-the-making, the life of the cutoff that leads to the estrangement, and the effect of a cutoff on the family. We have investigated remedies for these. We have seen why the final break feels to be the only true course and inevitable to the person doing it, and why the cutoff is irreversible at that point. This is all true of mass populations of cutoffs as well. The problem is how to reach these people.

Cutting off is a kind of separation that doesn't usually work, because it omits closure on the old love or the old life and has a half-life all its own in succeeding generations. The dilemma is that the traumas themselves—including death and loss—evoke so many conflicted feelings at the time they are occurring that cutting off feels like the least painful way out.

On the other hand, if one is actively involved in the search for closure, it matters that someone who cares whether you reconnect or not is standing by. A search for an ending means allowing for unpleasant feelings as they arise, staying with them, turning them over in the mind, and, finally, integrating them. But that search eventually leads to a sense of completion, and there is a gratified sense that the job is over and done.

Some cutoffs are resistant to any reversal because the person cutting off feels brutalized by another family member. This is certainly true in the case of child abuse and feels the same when a woman claims incest, falsely. In these cases where the basis of trust is gone, there is hardly any hope for reconciliation. In one instance, the woman has been violated by her father; in the other, the woman has violated her father. Any attempt at reconciliation is futile, unless it begins with the admission that trust is gone and that the first order of business is to try to rebuild it.

A feeling of profound invasion, whether true or only perceived, is common to all absolute cutoffs. Melitta Schmideberg, Melanie Klein's daughter whose story was told earlier, described exactly what it was like when she accused her mother of "trying to force feelings into me." That was her perception of what happened but it felt like an actual violation. It felt real, and it was the perceived reality she acted on.

Also, an actual invasion of one kind can be converted into

a feeling of invasion of another kind. For example, Fran was physically forced to have an abortion when she was a teenager. Her parents and extended relatives pushed her into a car, held her down, and carried her into the clinic. For her, this forced entry into her body became one of the building blocks of false memory about incest. The invasion felt like rape by family which is exactly what she claimed to have happened when she was in the recovered-memory movement. A true experience of physical and emotional abuse metamorphosed into one of sexual abuse, and years later she punished family and neighbors by pressing charges against them, but for the wrong crime. Although she forgot the abortion, the feeling of having been invaded persisted, and was so real, so strong, so imperative, this retractor now says, that she acted on it.

Reconnection with an absolute cutoff means providing a holding pattern, from a distance, for extreme cutoffs feel invaded or overtaken and will not allow anyone near. As was said in the chapter on reconnection, the goal is to enter the foyer of consciousness over time. This is slow work because, for the cutoff, those left behind do not exist as real persons.

In the case of Ellen and Meg, for example, Ellen refused a final break for many years and reminded Meg that she was there in small ways until Meg finally began to recognize her mother's real qualities again, also in very small ways. The process took years, but it worked. Even with absolute cutoffs, transferences are reversible and reconnection is possible, but movement is often slow. All families, even "good" ones, have many undercurrents, including hidden alliances, that resist movement. These collusive alliances strengthen a cutoff from within. However, even in those cases, somewhere in the family there is often a counterbalance, and a cutoff can be undermined from without. For example, Olivia McKillop, who falsely accused family members of incest and later retracted these accusations, had skeptical friends who challenged her. Finally, after the ten-year-old child who was a real incest victim told her about it, Olivia was ready to hear her friends. Meg's brother David wrote to her regularly during the years she was cut off, and although she never replied, when she was ready to come back in the family she moved toward him first.

The model for repairing any cutoff, including mass cut-offs, is the investment of one person in another. The deepest sense of closure comes from dealing literally with the facts of the past no matter how grim or difficult. To heal, there is now a psychological need for the real. This is best done with the sense of a benevolent presence nearby. The reason is that although connection is always the solution for cutoff and is worth any effort, retrieving a cutoff is hard work. The sense that someone is standing by to help is a reminder that connection matters and helps sustain the effort.

REFERENCES

Advocates For Youth (AFY). (1994). Adolescent sexual behavior, pregnancy, and parenthood. Washington, DC. Jan.

Ahrons, C. A. (1994). *The good divorce*. New York: HarperCollins.

Baran, A., and Panoor, R. (1990). Open adoption. In Brodzinsky, 1990.

Bass, Ellen, and Davis, Laura. (1994). *The courage to heal*. 3d ed. New York: Harper Perennial.

Bion, W. R. (1962). *Learning from experience*. New York: Basic Books.

Bollas, Christopher. (1995). A mind gone mad: From compulsion to hallucination. Lecture, Institute and Society for Contemporary Psychotherapy conference, *The mind object* (18 Feb.).

———. (1989). *Forces of destiny*. London: Free Association.

———. (1987). *The shadow of the object*. New York: Columbia University Press.

Bowlby, John. (1991). *Charles Darwin: A new life*. New York: W. W. Norton.

Brinich, Paul. (1990). Adoption from the inside out: A psychoanalytic perspective. In Brodzinsky, 1990, pp. 42-61.

Brodkey, Harold. (1992, September 7). Mia Farrow: A Jewish Hemingway and the peculiar ties of adoption. *New York Observer*.

————. (1988a). Largely an oral history of my mother. *Stories in an almost classical mode.* New York: Knopf.

————. (1988b). Ceil. *Stories.*

————. (1988c). S.L. *Stories.*

Brodzinsky, David, and Schechter, Marshall, D., eds. (1990). *The psychology of adoption.* New York: Oxford University Press. Quoting Doris Bertocci and Marshall D. Schechter, "The meaning of the search," pp. 62-69; and Ann Hartman and Joan Laird, "Family treatment after adoption: Common themes," pp. 221-239.

Centers for Disease Control (CDC). (1992). Sexual behavior among high school students, United States, 1990. *Morbidity and Mortality Weekly Report, 40*(51, 52) (3 Jan.).

Crews, Frederick. (1994, December 1). Victims of repressed memory. *New York Review of Books.* Pt. 2.

Davidson, Howard. (1992, September 21). Irreconcilable differences. *Newsweek,* pp. 84-90. (Special report 21.) Speaking on behalf of the American Bar Association on children and the law.

Dissociation and dissociative disorders. (1992, April). *Harvard Mental Health Letter,* 8(10). Cambridge.

Faludi, Susan. (1991). *Backlash.* New York: Crown.

Freud, Sigmund. (1905). *A case of hysteria.* SE, 7.

————. (1930). *Civilization and its discontents.* SE, 21.

Gavigan, Melody. *The Retractors' Newsletter.*

Gelderman, Carol. (1988). *Mary McCarthy: A life.* New York: St. Martin's Press.

Grosskurth, P. (1987). *Melanie Klein: Her world and her work.* Cambridge: Harvard University Press.

Hubbell, Sue. (1986). *A country year.* New York: Harper and Row.

Jacobson, E. (1965). The return of the lost parent. In *Drives, affects, behavior,* vol. 2, ed. M. Schurr, pp. 193-211. New York: International Universities Press.

Jahanbegloo, R. (1992, May 28). Philosophy and life: An interview with Isaiah Berlin. *New York Review of Books.*

References

Kane, Frank. (1995, March). Working together. *FMSF Newsletter.*

Kernberg, Paulina. (1985). Child analysis with a severely disturbed adoptive child. *International Journal of Psychoanalytic Psychotherapy*, 2, 000-000.

Khan, Masud. (1988). *The privacy of the self.* New York: International Universities Press.

———. (1983). *Hidden selves.* London: Hogarth Press.

King, Pearl, and Steiner, Riccardo. (1991). *The Freud-Klein controversies: 1941-45.* London: Routledge.

Kinsey, Alfred C., Martin, Clyde E., Pomeroy, Wardell B., and Gebhard, Paul H. et al. (1953). *Sexual behavior in the human female.* Philadelphia: W. B. Saunders.

Klein, Melanie. (1987). Notes on some schizoid mechanisms. In *The selected Melanie Klein*, ed. Juliet Mitchell. New York: Free Press.

Kundera, M. (1984). *The unbearable lightness of being.* New York: Harper and Row.

Lerner, Paul M. (1990). The treatment of early object loss: The need to search. In *Psychoanalytic Psychology,* 7(1), 79-91.

Lifton, Betty Jean. (1994). *Journey for the adopted self: A quest for wholeness.* New York: Basic Books.

Lifton, Robert Jay. (1991, February). Cults. *Harvard Mental Health Letter,* 7(8). Cambridge.

Loftus, E. (1994). *The myth of repressed memory.* New York: St. Martin's Press.

McGoldrick, M., and Gerson, R. (1985). *Genograms in family assess ment.* New York: W. W. Norton.

McHugh, Paul. (1992). Psychiatric misadventures. *The American Scholar*, 61(4), 497-510.

May, Robert. (1980). *Sex and fantasy.* New York: W. W. Norton.

The meeting was fine. (1995, March). *FMSF Newsletter.*

Meissner, W. W. (1978). *The paranoid process.* Northvale, NJ: Jason Aronson.

Melina, Lois Ruskai. (1990a, March). Adoption rituals needed to enhance sense of "family." *Adopted Child.*

———. (1990b, November). Waiting parents must prepare for child physically and psychologically. *Adopted Child.*

———. (1988, September). Open adoptions require building

relationships. *Adopted Child.*

———. (1984, June). Even babies can have adjustment problems. *Adopted Child.*

———. (1982, January). Bonding: A lifelong experience. *Adopted Child.*

Melina, Lois, and Roszia, Sharon. (1993). *The open adoption experience.* New York: Harper Perennial.

Modell, A. (1990). *Other times, other realities: Toward a theory of psychoanalytic treatment.* Cambridge: Harvard University Press.

———. (1984). *Psychoanalysis in a new context.* New York: International Universities Press.

Moore, B. E., and Fine, B. (1983). *A glossary of psychoanalytic terms and concepts.* New York: American Psychoanalytic Association.

Moore, Thomas. (1991). *Care of the soul.* New York: HarperCollins.

Novick, Jack. (1990). Masochism and the delusion of omnipotence. Paper, American Psychological Association, Division 39, April 8, New York.

Ofshe, Richard, and Watters, Ethan. (1994). *Making monsters.* New York: Scribner's.

Ogden, Thomas. (1989). *The primitive edge of experience.* Northvale, NJ: Jason Aronson.

———. (1986). *The matrix of the mind.* Northvale, NJ: Jason Aronson. Quoting Bion, 1962, p. 34.

Pendergrast, Mark. (1995). *Victims of memory: Incest accusations and shattered lives.* Hinesburg, VT: Upper Access Press.

Porter, Bruce. (1993, April 11). I met my daughter at the Wuhan Foundling Hospital. *New York Times Magazine.*

Rangell, Leo. (1985). The object in psychoanalytic theory. *Journal of the American Psychoanalytic Association, 33,* 301-310.

Retraction is a process and not an event. (1995, January). *FMSF Newsletter.*

Rosenfeld, H. (1987). *Impasse and interpretation.* London: Tavistock.

Rush, Norman. (1991). *Mating.* New York: Knopf.

References

Sandalowski, M., B. G. Harris, and Holditch-Davis, D. (1993, January). Somewhere out there. *Journal of Contemporary Ethnography, 21*(4), 464-487.

Schmideberg, Melitta. (1936). *International Journal of Psychoanalysis, 17,* 1-5.

Seinfeld, J. (1990). *The bad object.* Northvale, NJ: Jason Aronson.

Sheehan, Susan. (1988, October 17). A German family. (A Reporter at Large.) *New Yorker,* 43-84.

———. (1993, January 11). A lost childhood. (A Reporter at Large.) *New Yorker,* 54-85.

Stassinopoulos-Huffington, A. (1988). *Picasso: Creator and destroyer.* New York: Simon and Schuster.

Stierlin, Helmut. (1977). *Psychoanalysis and family therapy: Selected papers.* Northvale, NJ: Jason Aronson.

Susser, Ezra S., Lin, Shang P., and Conover, Sarah A. (1991, December). Risk factors for homelessness among patients admitted to a state mental hospital. *American Journal of Psychiatry, 148,* 1659-1664.

Susser, Ezra S., Lin, Shang P., Conover, Sarah A., and Struening, Elmer L. (1991, August). Childhood antecedents of homeless-- ness in psychiatric patients. *American Journal of Psychiatry, 148,* 1026-1030.

Tyson, Phyllis, and Tyson, Robert L. (1990). *Psychoanalytic theories of development: An integration.* New Haven: Yale University Press.

Visher, John, and Visher, Emily. (1988). *Old loyalties, new ties.* New York: Brunner Mazel.

Wallerstein, Judith, and Blakeslee, Sandra. (1989). *Second chances: Men, women, and children a decade after divorce.* New York: Ticknor & Fields.

Wilson, James Q. (1994). From welfare reform to character development. 1994 Wriston Lecture, Manhattan Institute for Policy Analysis. New York: MIPA.

Winnicott, D. W. (1991). *Playing and reality.* London: Routledge.

———. (1984). The family and individual development. London: Tavistock.

Wolff, E. (1987). *Emily Dickinson.* New York: Knopf.

Young-Breuhl, Elisabeth. (1988). *Anna Freud.* New York: Summit
Books.